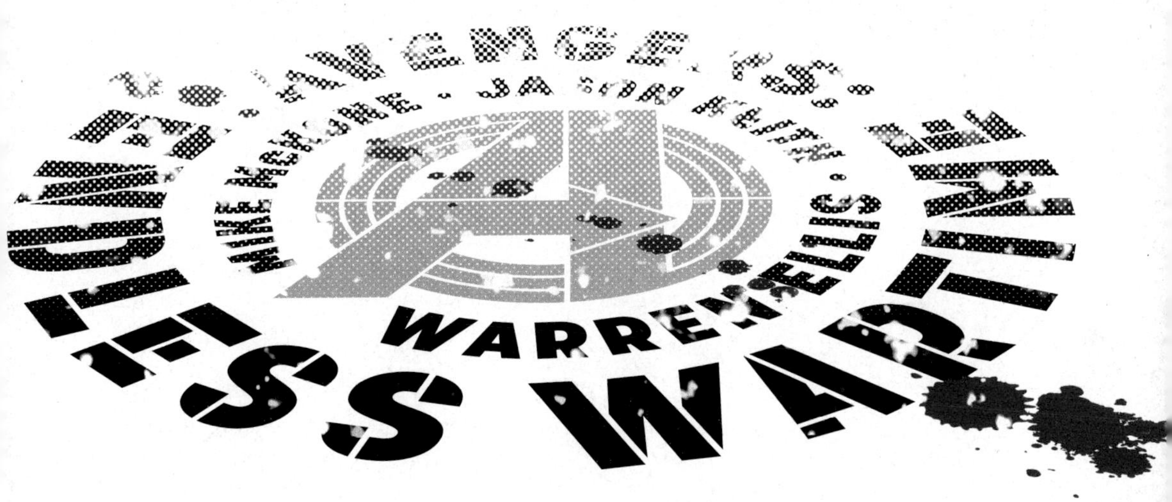
MIKE MCKONE
WARREN ELLIS

AVENGERS: ENDLESS WARTIME
First printing 2016.
ISBN# 978-0-7851-8468-3.
Published by MARVEL WORLDWIDE, INC.,
a subsidiary of MARVEL ENTERTAINMENT, LLC.
OFFICE OF PUBLICATION:
135 West 50th Street, New York, NY 10020.
Copyright © 2016 MARVEL

Printed in the U.S.A.
ALAN FINE, President, Marvel Entertainment;
DAN BUCKLEY, President, TV, Publishing &
Brand Management;
JOE QUESADA, Chief Creative Officer;
TOM BREVOORT, SVP of Publishing;
DAVID BOGART, SVP of Business Affairs &
Operations, Publishing & Partnership;
C.B. CEBULSKI, VP of Brand Management &
Development, Asia;
DAVID GABRIEL, SVP of Sales & Marketing, Publishing;
JEFF YOUNGQUIST, VP of Production & Special Projects;
DAN CARR, Executive Director of Publishing Technology;
ALEX MORALES, Director of Publishing Operations;
SUSAN CRESPI, Production Manager;
STAN LEE, Chairman Emeritus.
For information regarding advertising in Marvel Comics
or on Marvel.com, please contact Vit DeBellis, Integrated
Sales Manager, at vdebellis@marvel.com.
For Marvel subscription inquiries,
please call 888-511-5480.
**Manufactured between 11/4/2016 and
12/12/2016 by QUAD/GRAPHICS
WASECA, WASECA, MN, USA.**

10 9 8 7 6 5 4 3 2 1

Warren Ellis
Author

Mike McKone
Illustrator

Jason Keith with Rain Beredo
Color Artists

VC's Chris Eliopoulos
Lettering

Rian Hughes
Book Design

Jake Thomas
Assistant Editor

Tom Brevoort with
Lauren Sankovitch
Editors

Axel Alonso
Editor In Chief

Joe Quesada
Chief Creative Officer

Dan Buckley
Publisher

Alan Fine
Executive Producer

Photo by Blake Gardner

It was my brother, Andrew, who first got me into comics. It was the '70s and I was buried in sci-fi novels - Bradbury, Asimov, Philip K. Dick - until the day Andrew walked through the door with an issue of *Iron Man* drawn by Jim Starlin. I peeled through the pages in awed silence. The stories were dark and powerful, but what took my breath away was the artwork - the detail, the worlds, the emotion etched onto faces. I bought more *Iron Man*, whose lack of super-powers and human frailty I found endlessly compelling. Soon I added *Luke Cage,* then *The Avengers,* and since Bruce Lee was our hero we both got heavily into *Iron Fist.* But my deepest passion was Starlin. I searched comic shops and garage sales for his 'books.' I found his *Daredevil* and *Captain Marvel* and became obsessed with *Warlock.* So obsessed, in fact, that when I recently dug up an old middle school notebook, the pages were so dominated by sketches of Adam Warlock that the school work was crammed into a few rumpled sheets in the back. Which is, of course, how one ends up with a career in the arts.

Many years later, I read that my neighbor, Jon Favreau, was

directing an origin movie of Iron Man, produced by Marvel with an amazing cast headed by Robert Downey Jr. as Tony Stark. I felt a rush of boyish excitement at the thought of even seeing the film. So when Jon offered me a minor role as a mysterious government agent named Coulson, the chance to interact with Tony Stark outside the pages of a spiral notebook was more than I could resist.

My first day on the film was like taking my 12-year-old self to work. I gaped at Robert's brilliant, razor-witted Tony Stark, but somehow managed to keep my geek-outs internal and even said most of my lines. When I got a call a few days later saying that they wanted to add more scenes for Agent Coulson, I quickly volunteered to clear my schedule. I soon found myself, as Agent Coulson, explaining to Tony Stark that I worked for "the Strategic Homeland Intervention Enforcement and Logistics Division." Between takes I asked young Marvel exec, Jeremy Latcham, if that acronym meant what I thought it meant. When Jeremy quietly confirmed my suspicion, I confessed to the twenty-five year gap in my Marvel timeline. The very next

day a thing of beauty arrived at my door - a thick, illustrated Iron Man 'bible' filled with chapters on Nick Fury, S.H.I.E.L.D. and the evolution of Tony Stark, including riveting panels from Warren Ellis' influential graphic novel, *Iron Man: Extremis.* As I curled up on a couch to pore through the encyclopedic tome, I half expected to hear my mother call me down to dinner.

Six years and one epic movie demise later, I'm still playing Agent Phil Coulson. My time with Marvel has given me an unusual opportunity to reconnect with boyhood heroes (often quite thrillingly in the flesh) and with the rich pop mythology that fills their stories. In addition, I've had the pleasure of watching Marvel and brilliant filmmakers like Jon Favreau, Kenneth Branagh and Joss Whedon bring those characters to cinematic life with a wit and sophistication that makes them as resonant and entertaining for me now as they were when I was a boy. So I was honored when Marvel asked me to write a forward to *Avengers: Endless Wartime,* a brilliant new graphic novel by Warren Ellis himself. *Avengers: Endless Wartime* is a

movie length epic that launches a new graphic novel line for Marvel with characters from the cinematic *Avengers,* like Captain America, Thor, Hawkeye, Black Widow and the Hulk, as well as beloved comic book Avengers like Wolverine and my personal favorite, the new female/alien incarnation of Captain Marvel. These Avengers are forced into combat with demons (quite literally) from Cap and Thor's shared past who turn out to be an unholy blend of cybernetic drone technology and a lost breed of Asgardian monsters.

Ellis is in prime form here and his crisp, edgy banter is brought to thrilling life by the incomparable panels of Mike McKone and the ensuing battle royal is even more badass than one might think possible. So, to Kevin Feige, Joe Quesada, Jeph Loeb and all the rest of my visionary friends at Marvel who, like me, never entirely grew up, thank you for once again pushing the envelope of your bold, imaginative world, and for giving me the opportunity to return to it.

Clark Gregg
June 16, 2013

Clark Gregg began his acting career as a founding member of the Atlantic Theater Company in NY, then moved to Los Angeles in the mid '90s where he landed roles in films including *Lovely and Amazing, In Good Company, Mr. Popper's Penguins, Thor, Iron Man* and *Iron Man 2, 500 Days of Summer, Marvel's The Avengers, The To Do List* and Joss Whedon's *Much Ado About Nothing.* On television he did recurring roles on *The West Wing, Sex and the City, Will and Grace* and co-starred with Julia Louis-Dreyfus on *The New Adventures of Old Christine.* Also a screenwriter and director, Gregg's screenwriting debut was *What Lies Beneath,* starring Harrison Ford and Michelle Pfeiffer. His directing debut, *Choke,* which he adapted from the novel by Chuck Palahniuk, won a special jury prize at the 2008 Sundance Film Festival. His second film, *Trust Me,* premiered at the 2013 Tribeca Film Festival. Gregg is poised to reprise his role of Agent Phil Coulson on *ABC's Marvel's Agents of S.H.I.E.L.D.*

INVENTORY

PART A · PART B · PART C · PART D · PART E · PART F · PART G · PART H · PART I · PART J · PART K · PART L · PART M · PART N · PART O · PART P · PART Q

TEAM MEMBER IDENTIFICATION

CAPTAIN AMERICA · THOR · IRON MAN

EMBLEM CONSTRUCTION

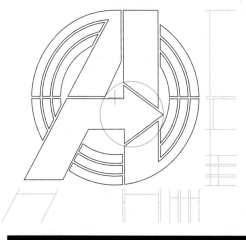

TYPEFACE: KOROLEV MILITARY STENCIL [includes international character set]

ABCDEFGHIJKLM
NOPQRSTUVWXYZ
aabcdefghijklmno
pqrstuvwxyz éëĕ
1234567890 ©®℗@
!@£$%^&*()-_+:;'"'<>?

10/13-A REV.2

These guidelines are here excerpted for informational purposes only.
Their use on any product or event implies no endorsement by The Avengers or their affiliates,
other than by prior arrangement via authorized agents. EAOE.
Please refer to the full Corporate Guidelines for detailed usage instructions.
Subject to change.

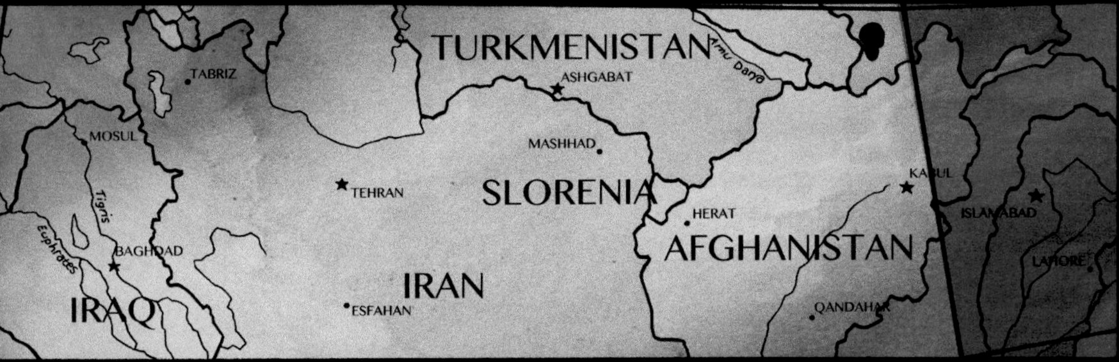
TURKMENISTAN
Amu Darya
ASHGABAT
TABRIZ
MOSUL
MASHHAD
TEHRAN
SLORENIA
KABUL
HERAT
ISLAMABAD
Tigris
Euphrates
BAGHDAD
AFGHANISTAN
LAHORE
IRAQ
IRAN
ESFAHAN
QANDAHAR

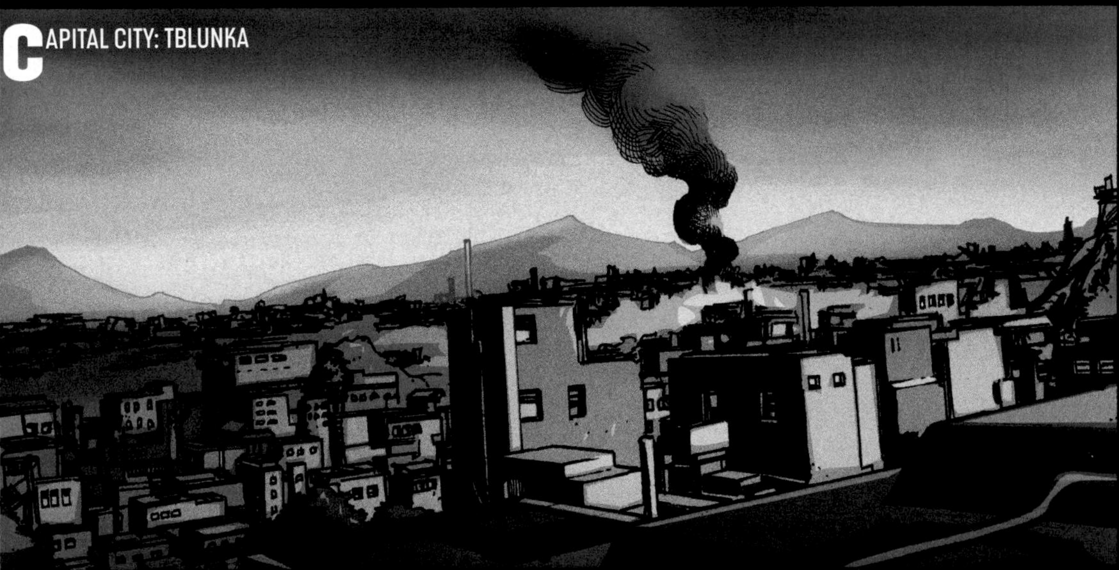
CAPITAL CITY: TBLUNKA

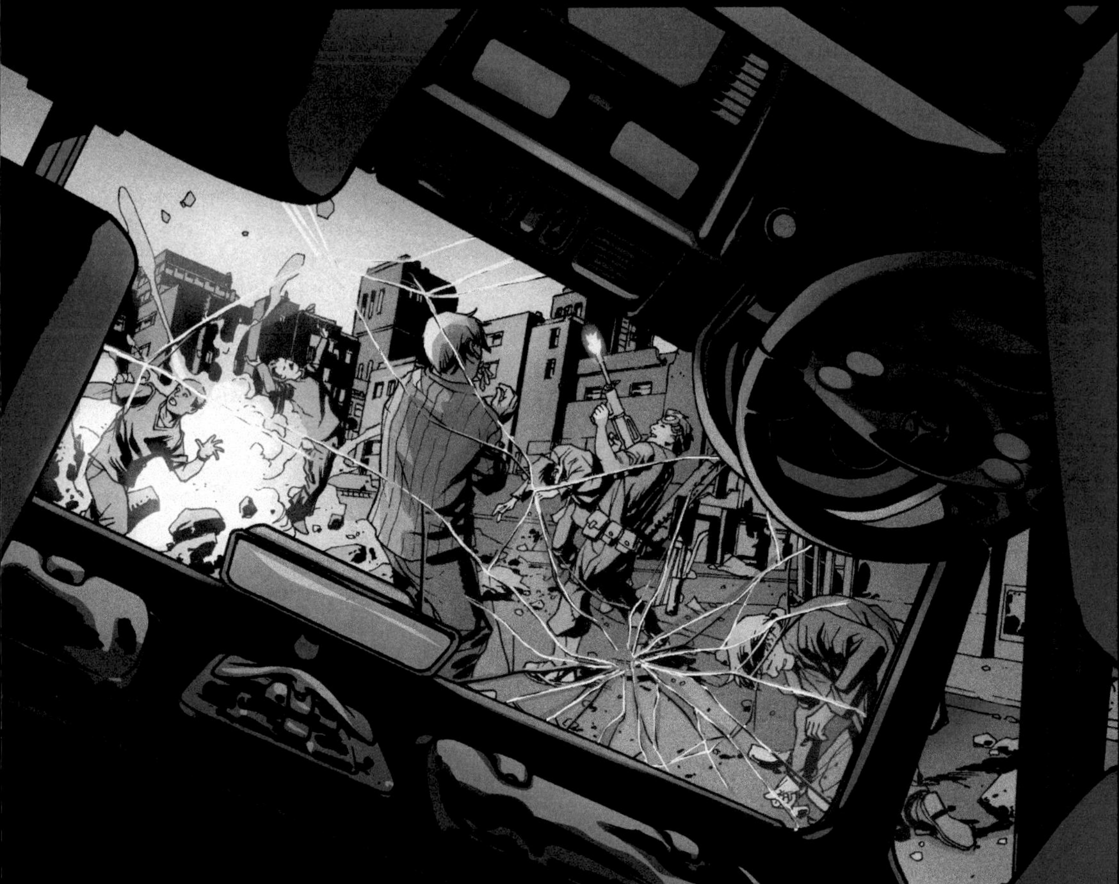

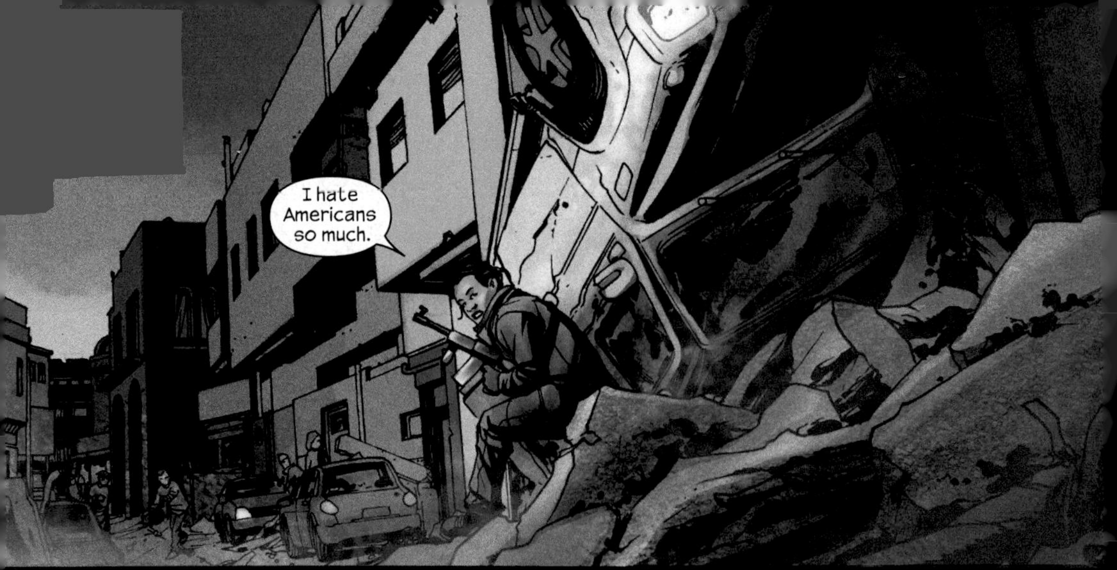
I hate Americans so much.

S.H.I.E.L.D.

S.H.I.E.L.D. HANDBOOK: SLORENIA [EXCERPT]

The unseated regime council, the Tabissara, formed a mercenary force (now also generically referred to as the Tabissara) to attempt to take Slorenia back from the democratically elected government. Given Slorenia's strategic position, military aid from America was swiftly forthcoming.

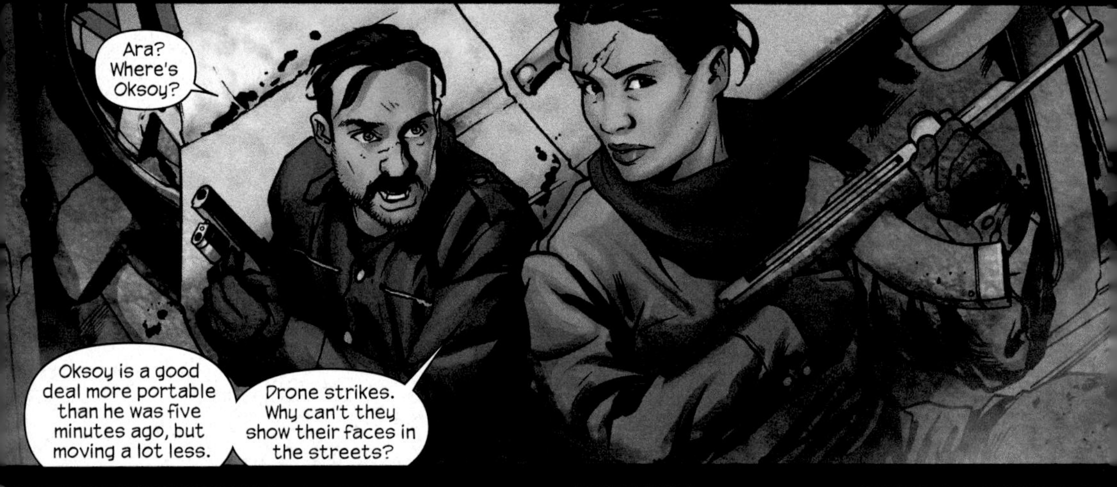
Ara? Where's Oksoy?
Oksoy is a good deal more portable than he was five minutes ago, but moving a lot less.
Drone strikes. Why can't they show their faces in the streets?

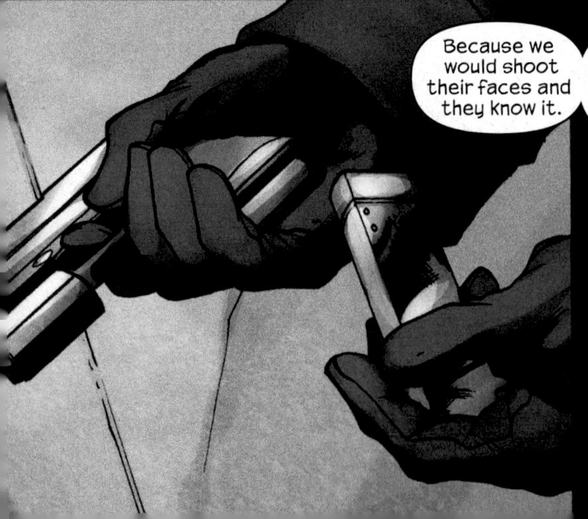
Because we would shoot their faces and they know it.

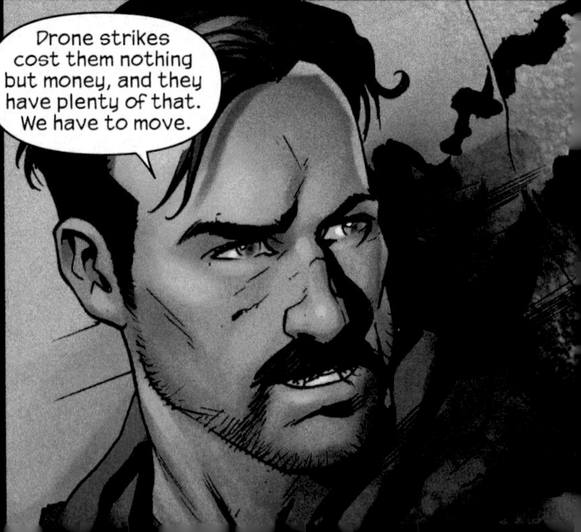
Drone strikes cost them nothing but money, and they have plenty of that. We have to move.

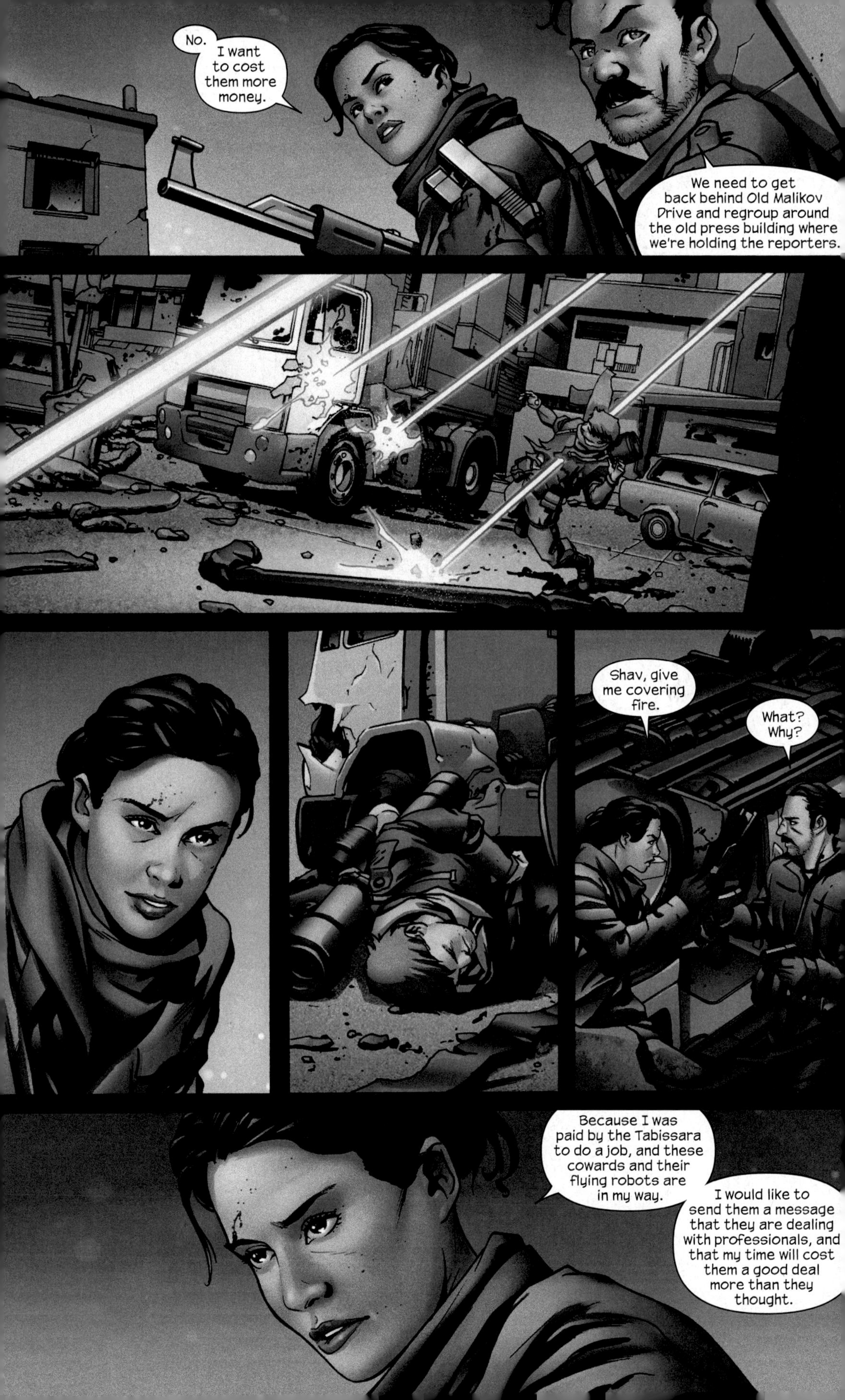
No. I want to cost them more money.
We need to get back behind Old Malikov Drive and regroup around the old press building where we're holding the reporters.
Shav, give me covering fire.
What? Why?
Because I was paid by the Tabissara to do a job, and these cowards and their flying robots are in my way.
I would like to send them a message that they are dealing with professionals, and that my time will cost them a good deal more than they thought.

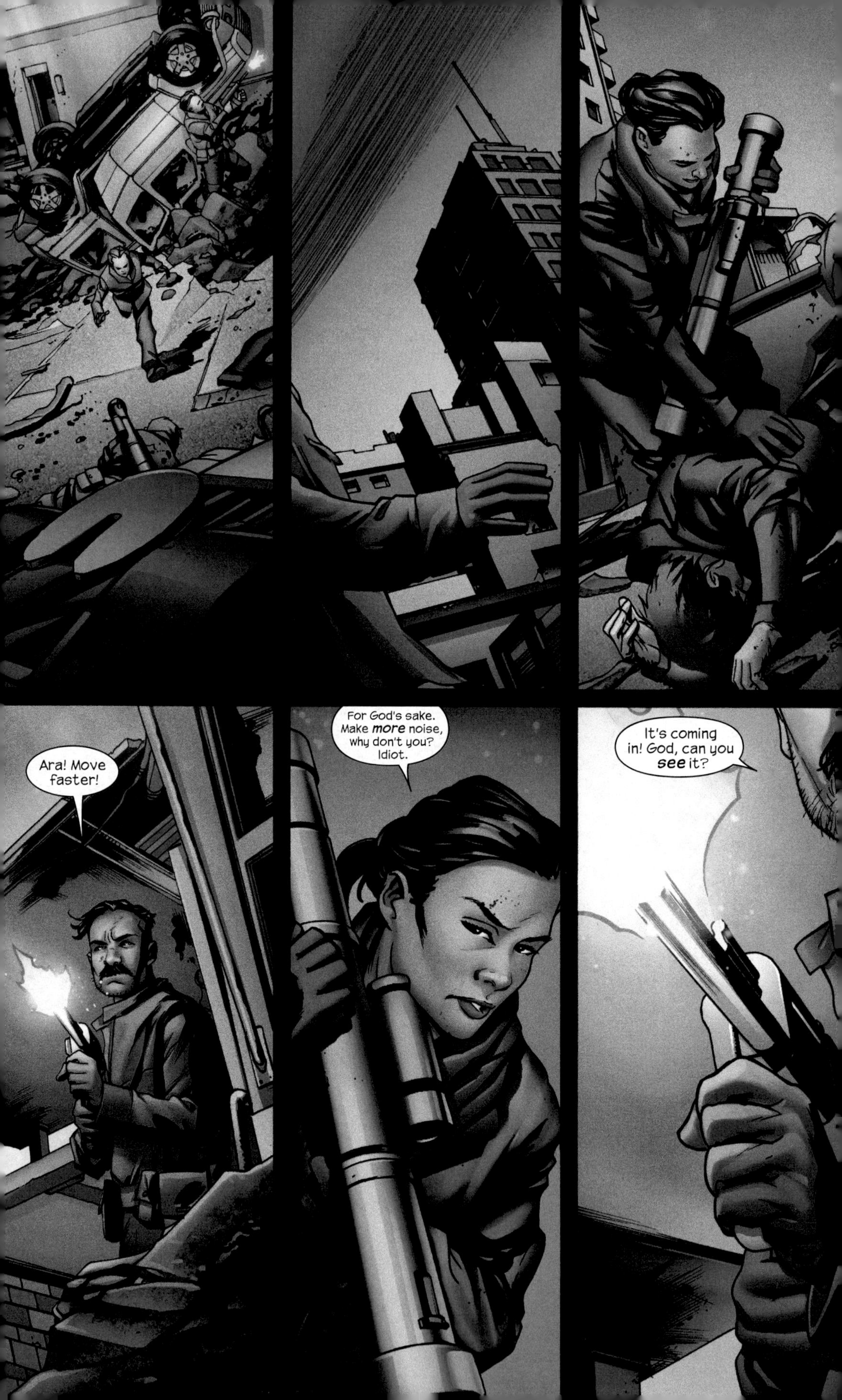
Ara! Move faster!
For God's sake. Make more noise, why don't you? Idiot.
It's coming in! God, can you see it?

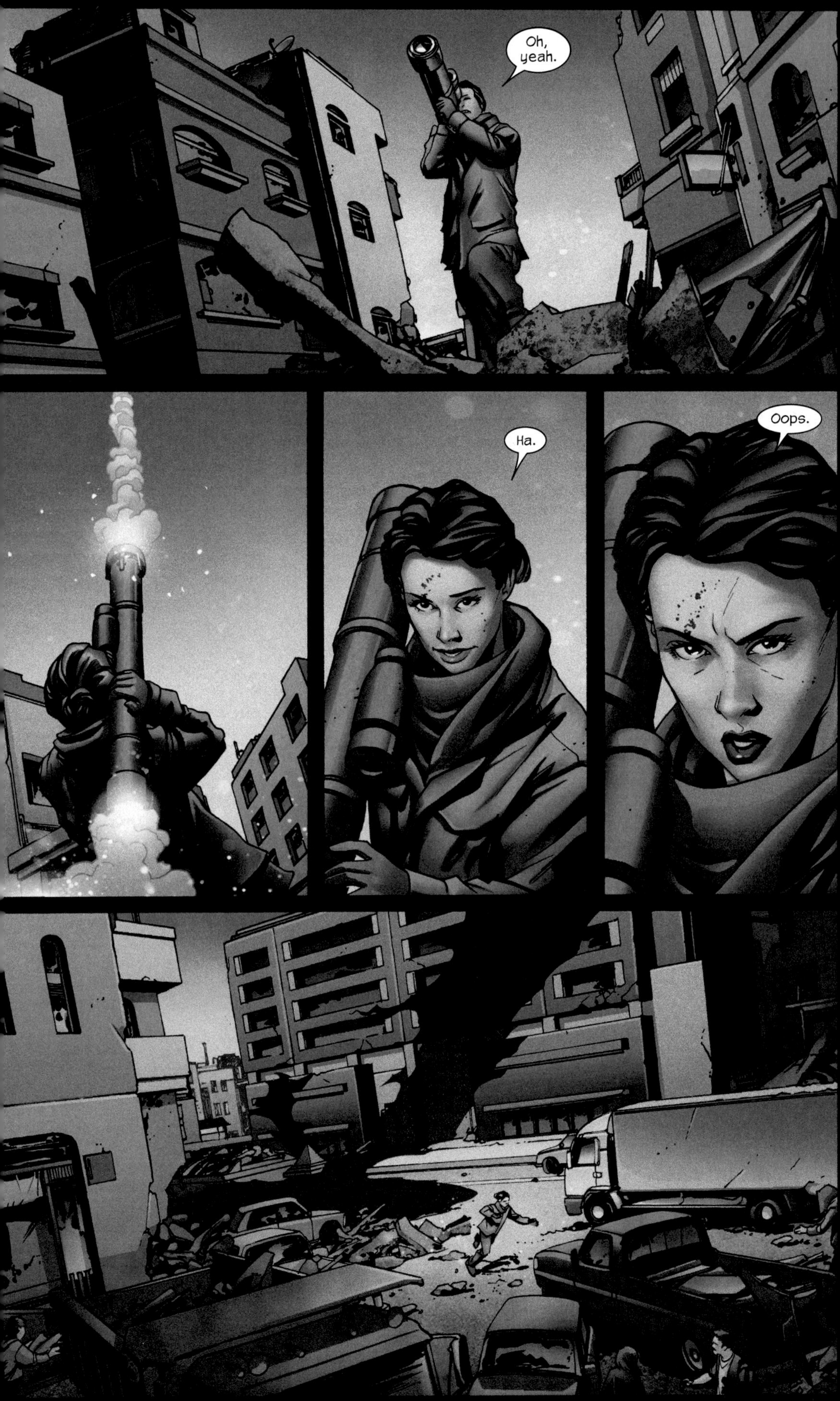
Oh, yeah.
Ha.
Oops.

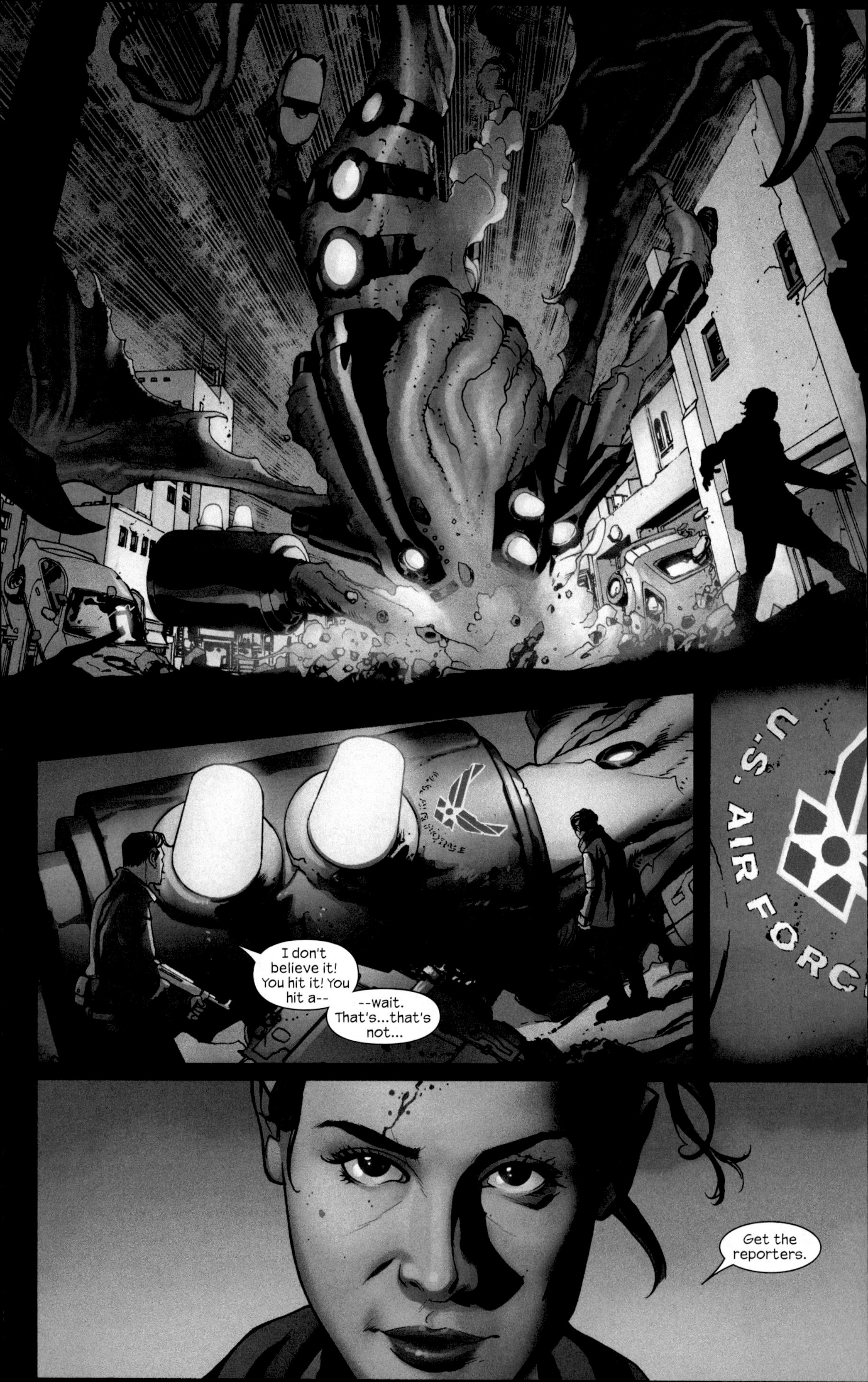
U.S. AIR FORC
I don't believe it! You hit it! You hit a--
--wait. That's...that's not...
Get the reporters.

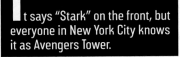

It says "Stark" on the front, but everyone in New York City knows it as Avengers Tower.

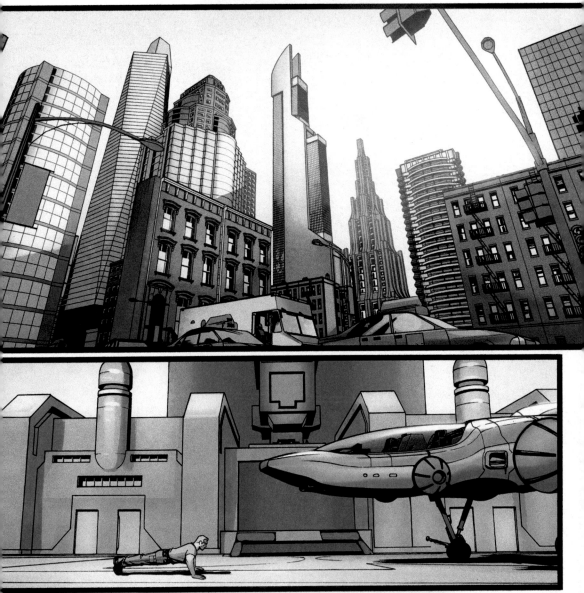

His name's Steve Rogers, but everyone knows him as Captain America, and the tower is home to him for part of each year.

As much as anything is home to him, even in part.

Even up here, he feels like he lives in a foreign country called The Future.

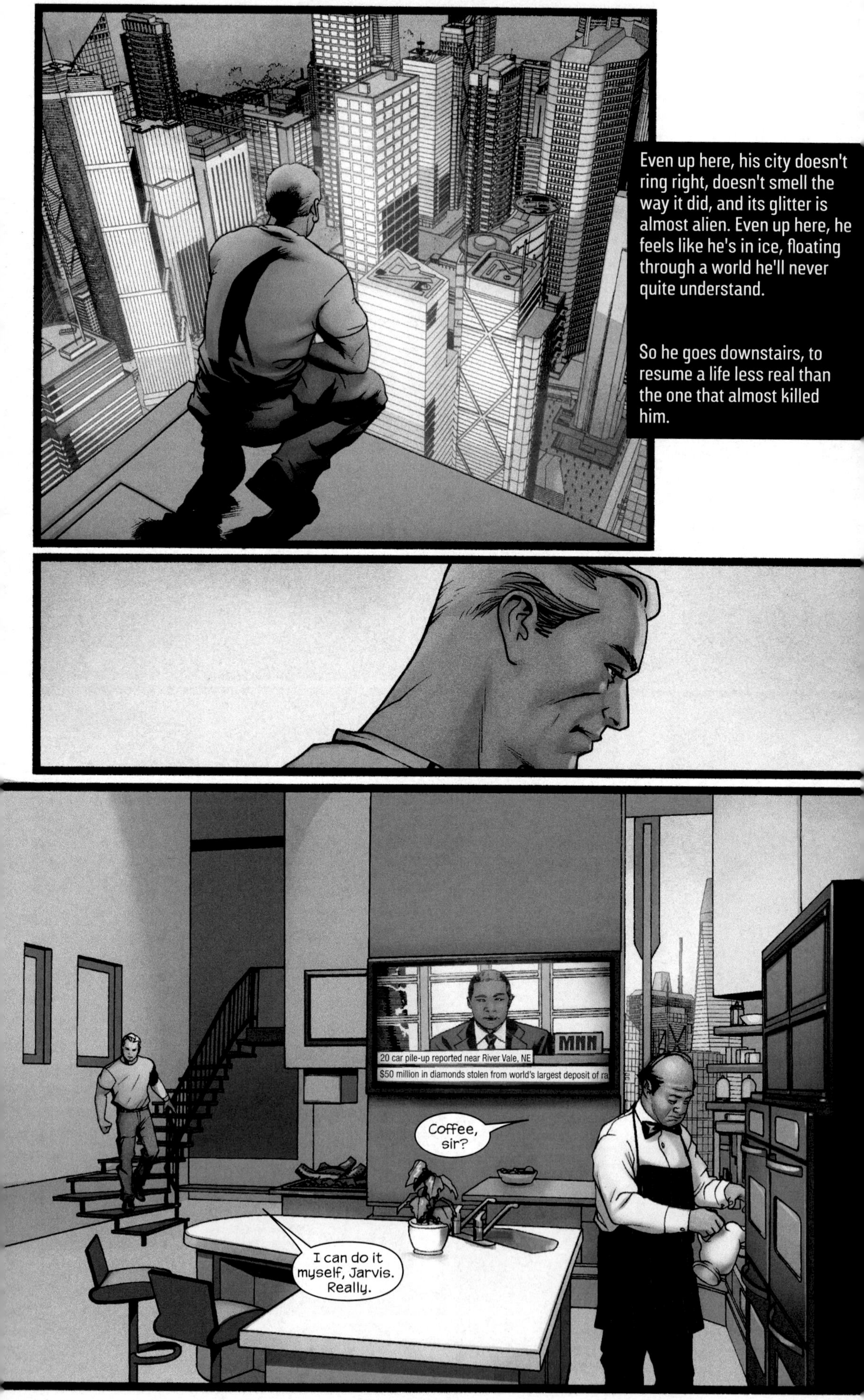

Even up here, his city doesn't ring right, doesn't smell the way it did, and its glitter is almost alien. Even up here, he feels like he's in ice, floating through a world he'll never quite understand.
So he goes downstairs, to resume a life less real than the one that almost killed him.
MNN
20 car pile-up reported near River Vale, NE
$50 million in diamonds stolen from world's largest deposit of ra
Coffee, sir?
I can do it myself, Jarvis. Really.

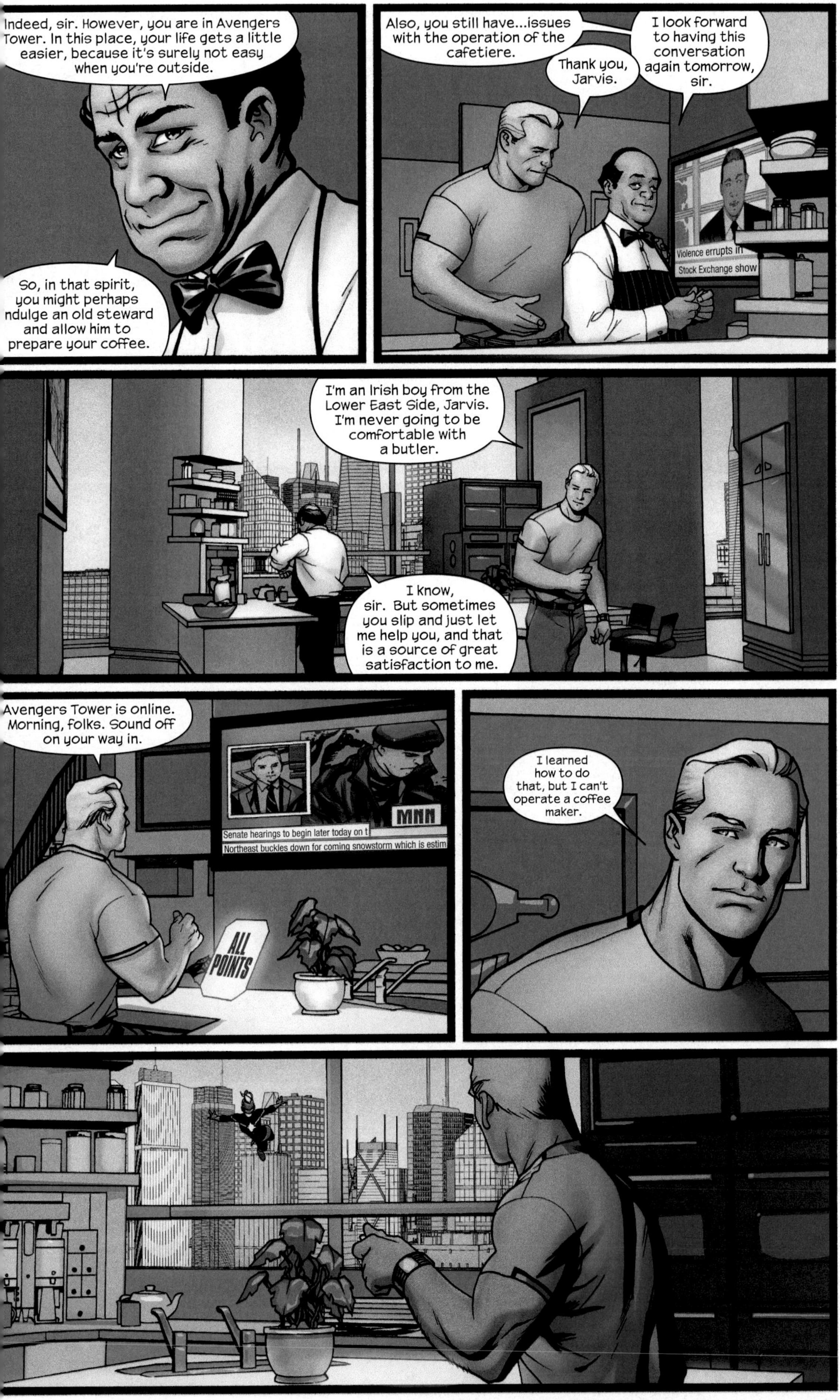
Indeed, sir. However, you are in Avengers Tower. In this place, your life gets a little easier, because it's surely not easy when you're outside.
So, in that spirit, you might perhaps ndulge an old steward and allow him to prepare your coffee.
Also, you still have...issues with the operation of the cafetiere.
Thank you, Jarvis.
I look forward to having this conversation again tomorrow, sir.
Violence errupts in
Stock Exchange show
I'm an Irish boy from the Lower East Side, Jarvis. I'm never going to be comfortable with a butler.
I know, sir. But sometimes you slip and just let me help you, and that is a source of great satisfaction to me.
Avengers Tower is online. Morning, folks. Sound off on your way in.
MNN
Senate hearings to begin later today on t
Northeast buckles down for coming snowstorm which is estim
ALL POINTS
I learned how to do that, but I can't operate a coffee maker.

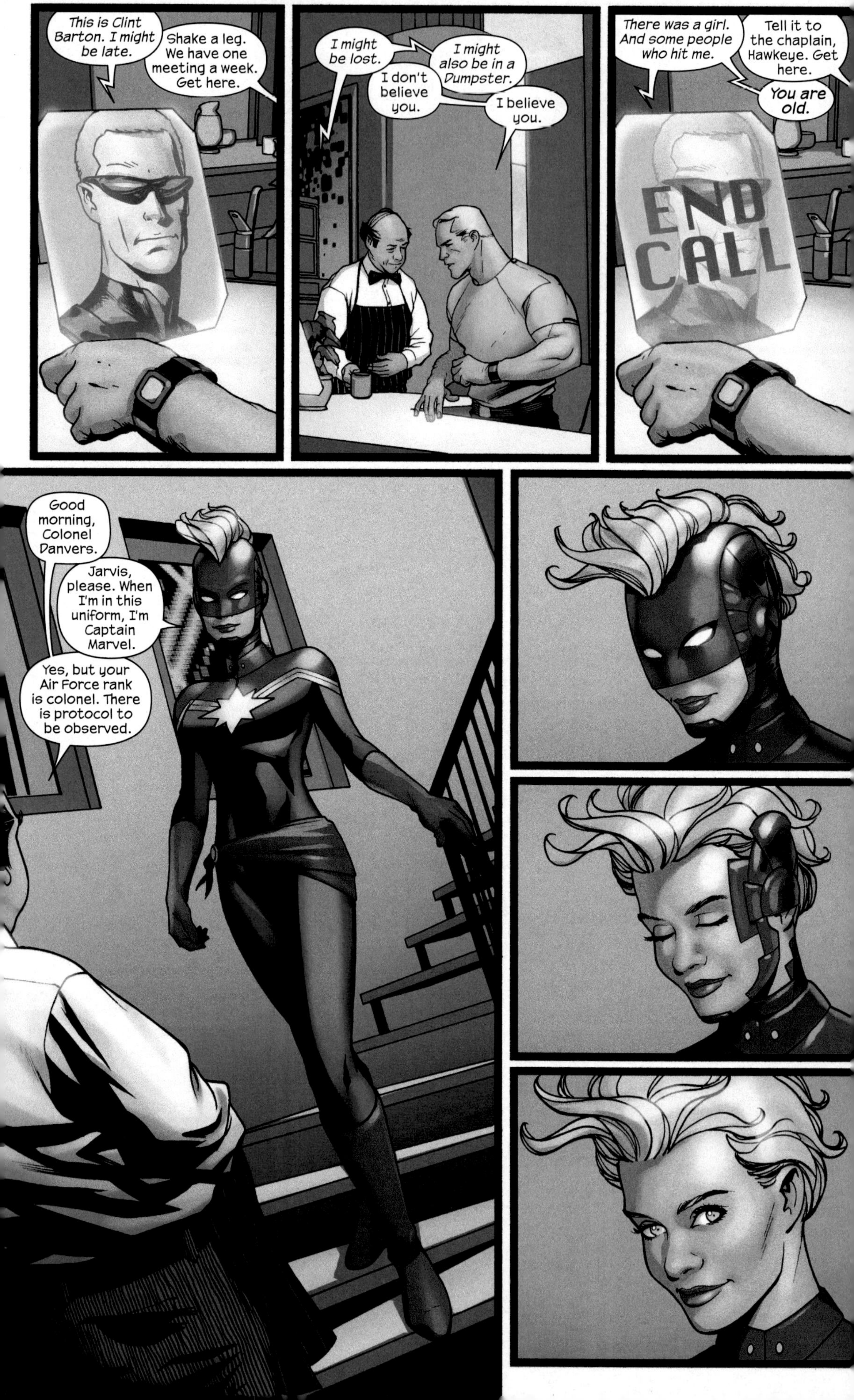

This is Clint Barton. I might be late.
Shake a leg. We have one meeting a week. Get here.
I might be lost.
I might also be in a Dumpster.
I don't believe you.
I believe you.
There was a girl. And some people who hit me.
Tell it to the chaplain, Hawkeye. Get here.
You are old.
END CALL
Good morning, Colonel Danvers.
Jarvis, please. When I'm in this uniform, I'm Captain Marvel.
Yes, but your Air Force rank is colonel. There is protocol to be observed.

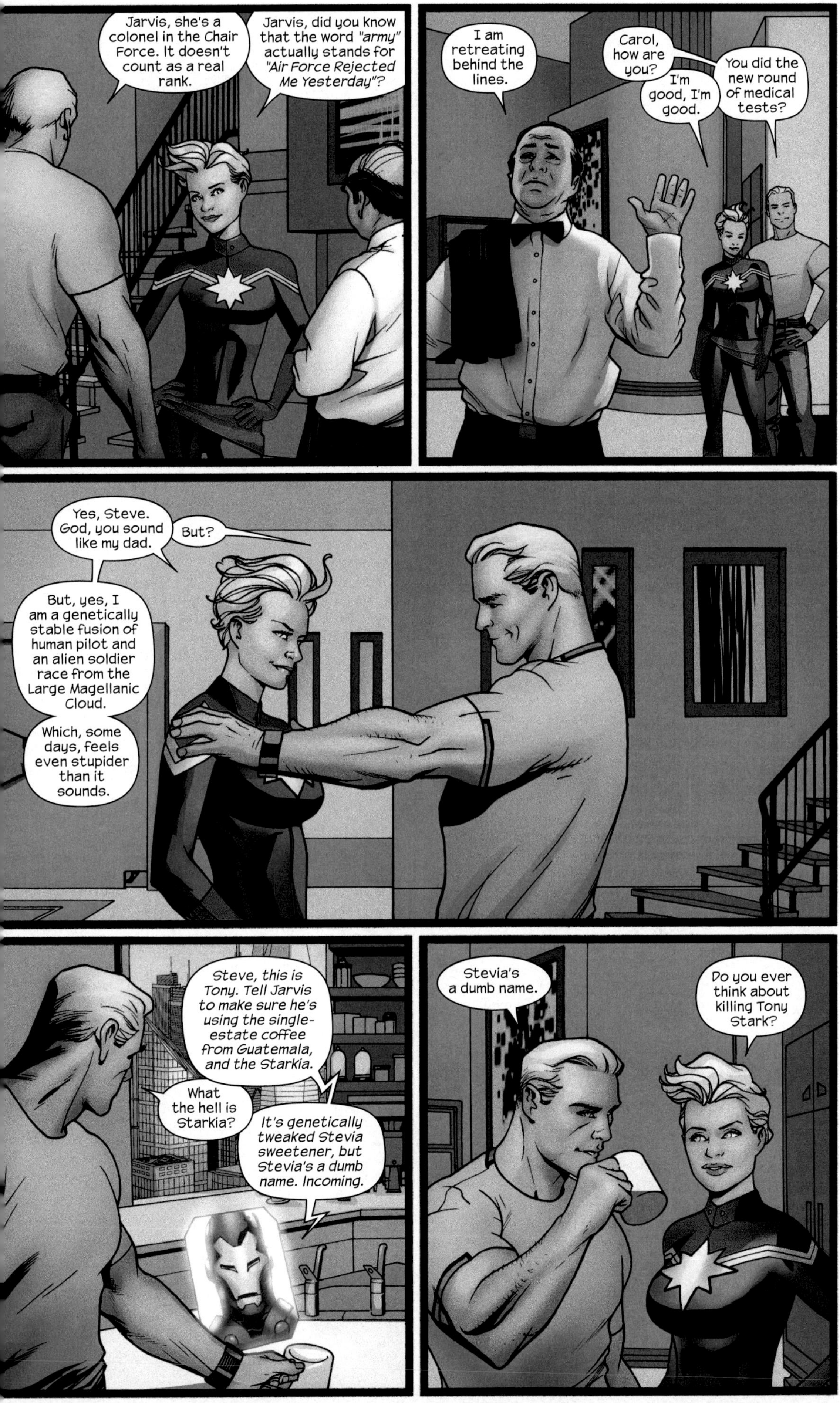

Jarvis, she's a colonel in the Chair Force. It doesn't count as a real rank.
Jarvis, did you know that the word "army" actually stands for "Air Force Rejected Me Yesterday"?
I am retreating behind the lines.
Carol, how are you?
You did the new round of medical tests?
I'm good, I'm good.
Yes, Steve. God, you sound like my dad.
But?
But, yes, I am a genetically stable fusion of human pilot and an alien soldier race from the Large Magellanic Cloud.
Which, some days, feels even stupider than it sounds.
Steve, this is Tony. Tell Jarvis to make sure he's using the single-estate coffee from Guatemala, and the Starkia.
What the hell is Starkia?
It's genetically tweaked Stevia sweetener, but Stevia's a dumb name. Incoming.
Stevia's a dumb name.
Do you ever think about killing Tony Stark?

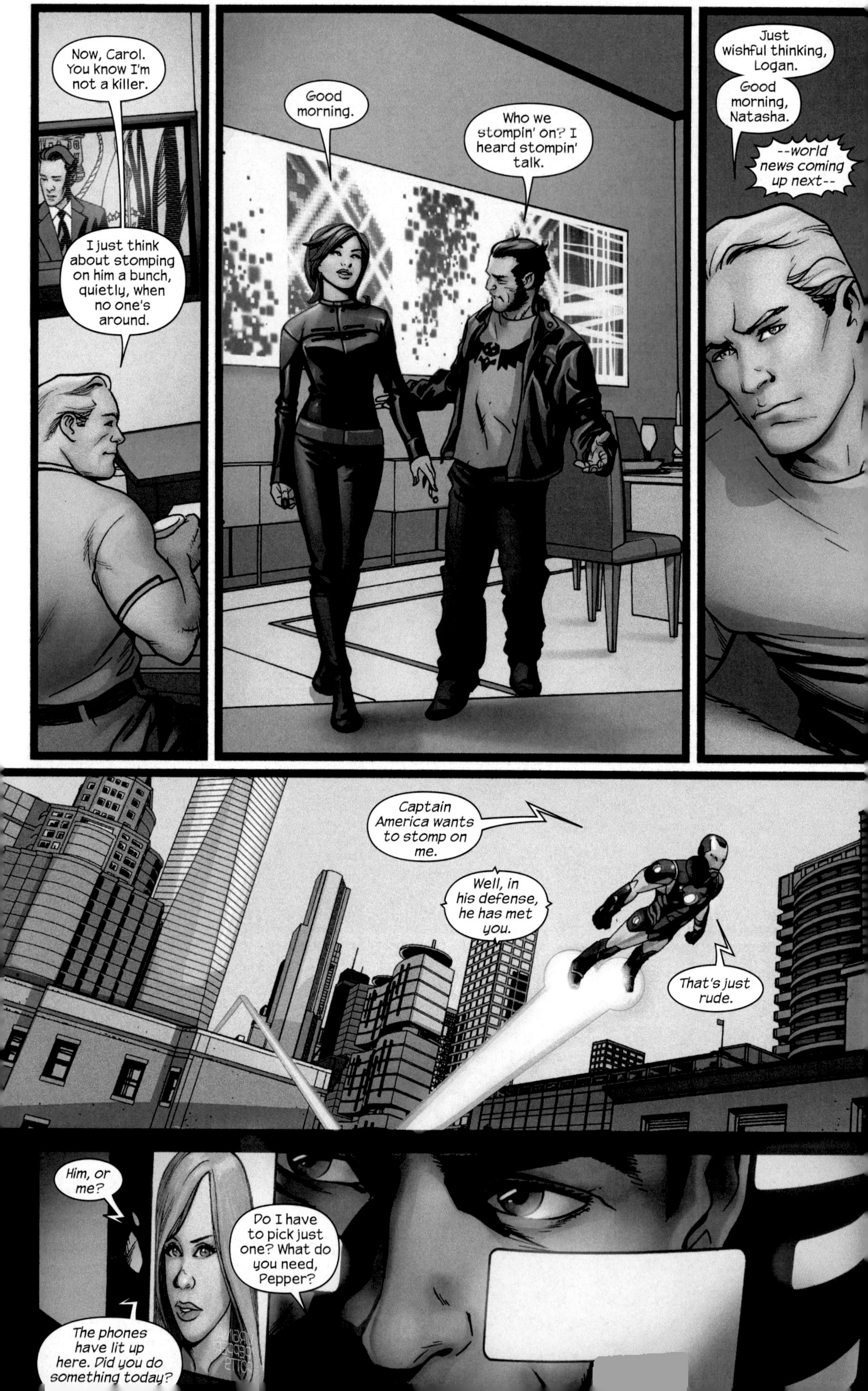
Now, Carol. You know I'm not a killer.
I just think about stomping on him a bunch, quietly, when no one's around.
Good morning.
Who we stompin' on? I heard stompin' talk.
Just wishful thinking, Logan.
Good morning, Natasha.
--world news coming up next--
Captain America wants to stomp on me.
Well, in his defense, he has met you.
That's just rude.
Him, or me?
Do I have to pick just one? What do you need, Pepper?
The phones have lit up here. Did you do something today?

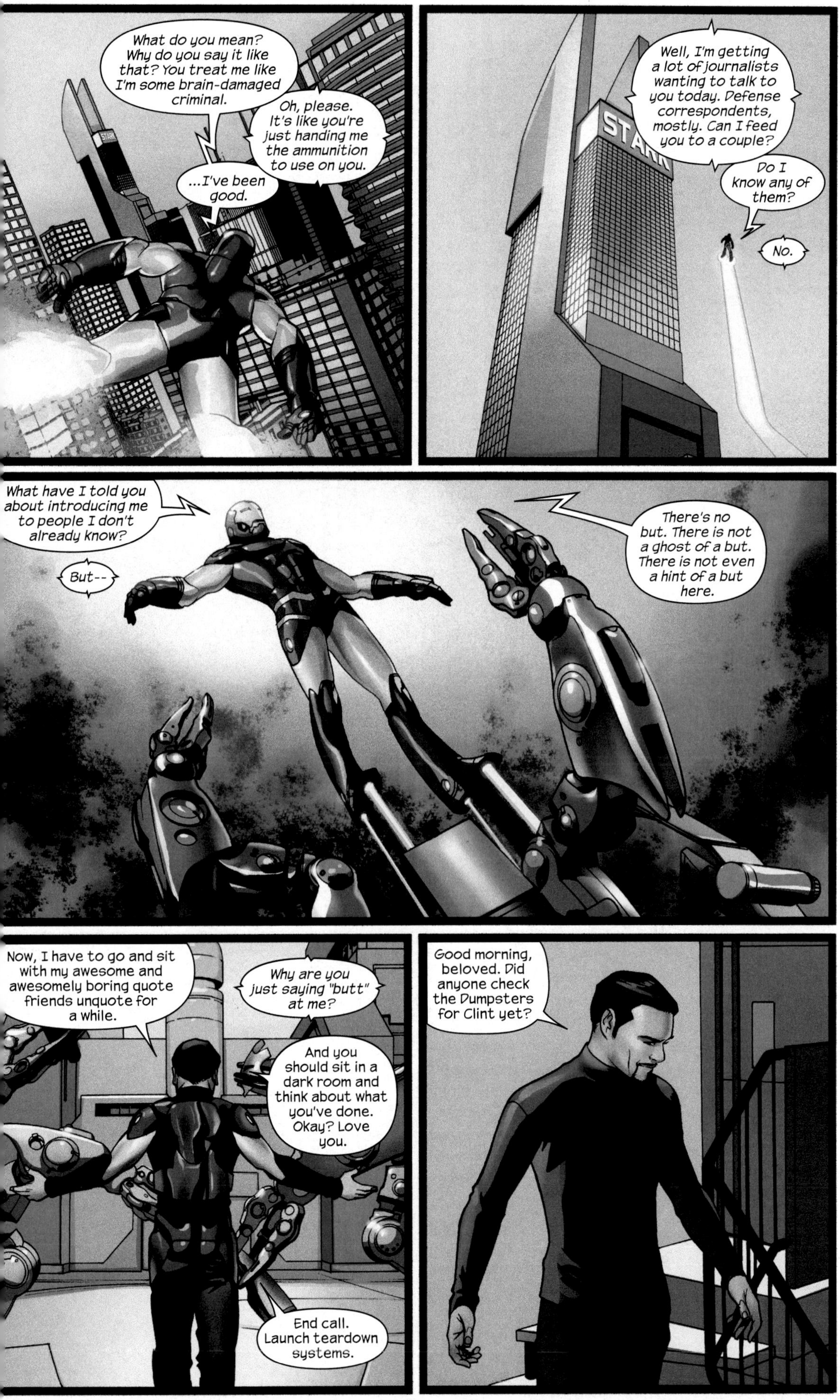
What do you mean? Why do you say it like that? You treat me like I'm some brain-damaged criminal.
Oh, please. It's like you're just handing me the ammunition to use on you.
...I've been good.
Well, I'm getting a lot of journalists wanting to talk to you today. Defense correspondents, mostly. Can I feed you to a couple?
Do I know any of them?
No.
What have I told you about introducing me to people I don't already know?
But--
There's no but. There is not a ghost of a but. There is not even a hint of a but here.
Now, I have to go and sit with my awesome and awesomely boring quote friends unquote for a while.
Why are you just saying "butt" at me?
And you should sit in a dark room and think about what you've done. Okay? Love you.
End call. Launch teardown systems.
Good morning, beloved. Did anyone check the Dumpsters for Clint yet?

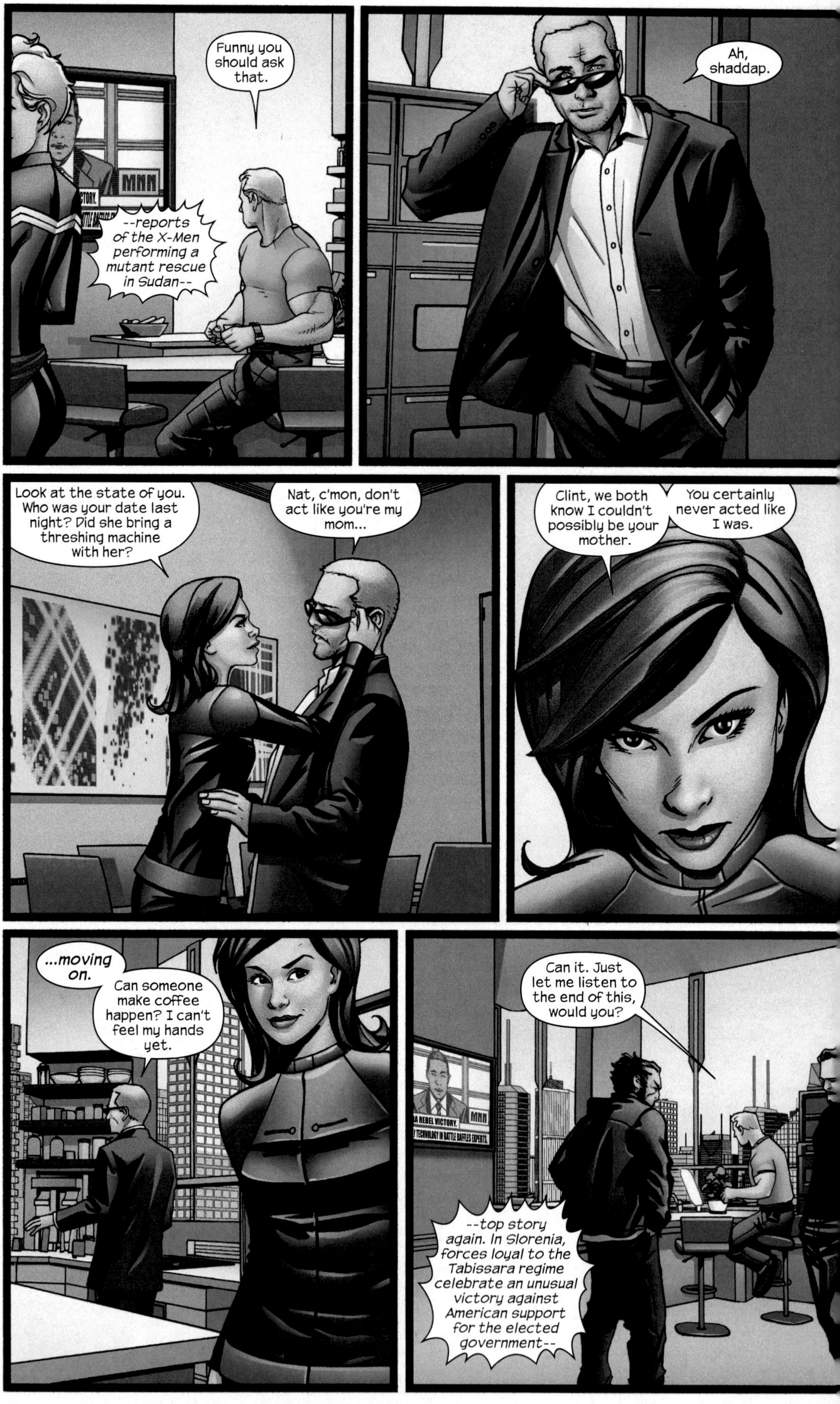

Funny you should ask that.
MNN
--reports of the X-Men performing a mutant rescue in Sudan--
Ah, shaddap.
Look at the state of you. Who was your date last night? Did she bring a threshing machine with her?
Nat, c'mon, don't act like you're my mom...
Clint, we both know I couldn't possibly be your mother.
You certainly never acted like I was.
...moving on.
Can someone make coffee happen? I can't feel my hands yet.
Can it. Just let me listen to the end of this, would you?
MNN
--top story again. In Slorenia, forces loyal to the Tabissara regime celebrate an unusual victory against American support for the elected government--

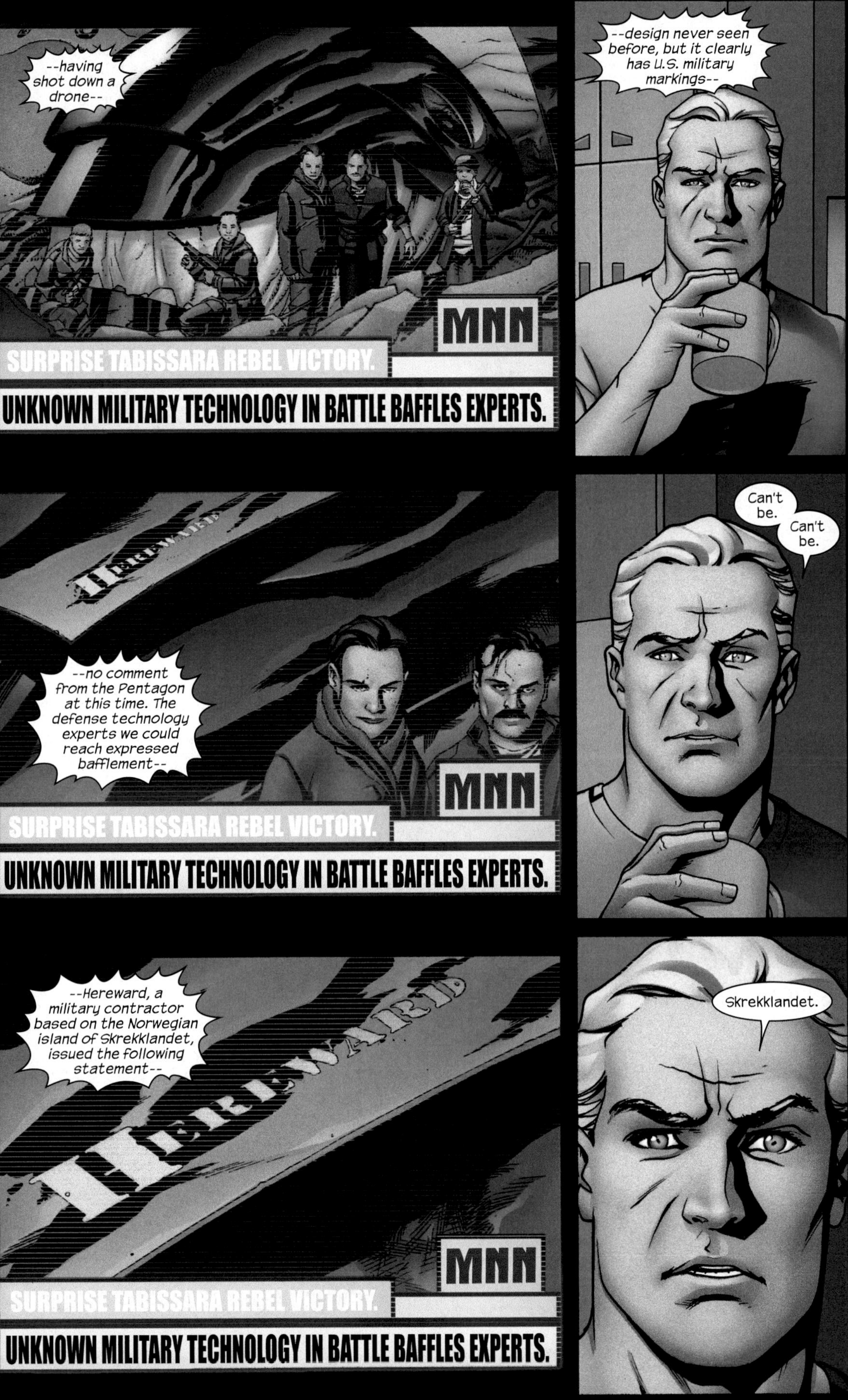
--having shot down a drone--
MNN
SURPRISE TABISSARA REBEL VICTORY.
UNKNOWN MILITARY TECHNOLOGY IN BATTLE BAFFLES EXPERTS.
--design never seen before, but it clearly has U.S. military markings--
HEREWARD
--no comment from the Pentagon at this time. The defense technology experts we could reach expressed bafflement--
MNN
SURPRISE TABISSARA REBEL VICTORY.
UNKNOWN MILITARY TECHNOLOGY IN BATTLE BAFFLES EXPERTS.
Can't be.
Can't be.
--Hereward, a military contractor based on the Norwegian island of Skrekklandet, issued the following statement--
HEREWARD
MNN
SURPRISE TABISSARA REBEL VICTORY.
UNKNOWN MILITARY TECHNOLOGY IN BATTLE BAFFLES EXPERTS.
Skrekklandet.

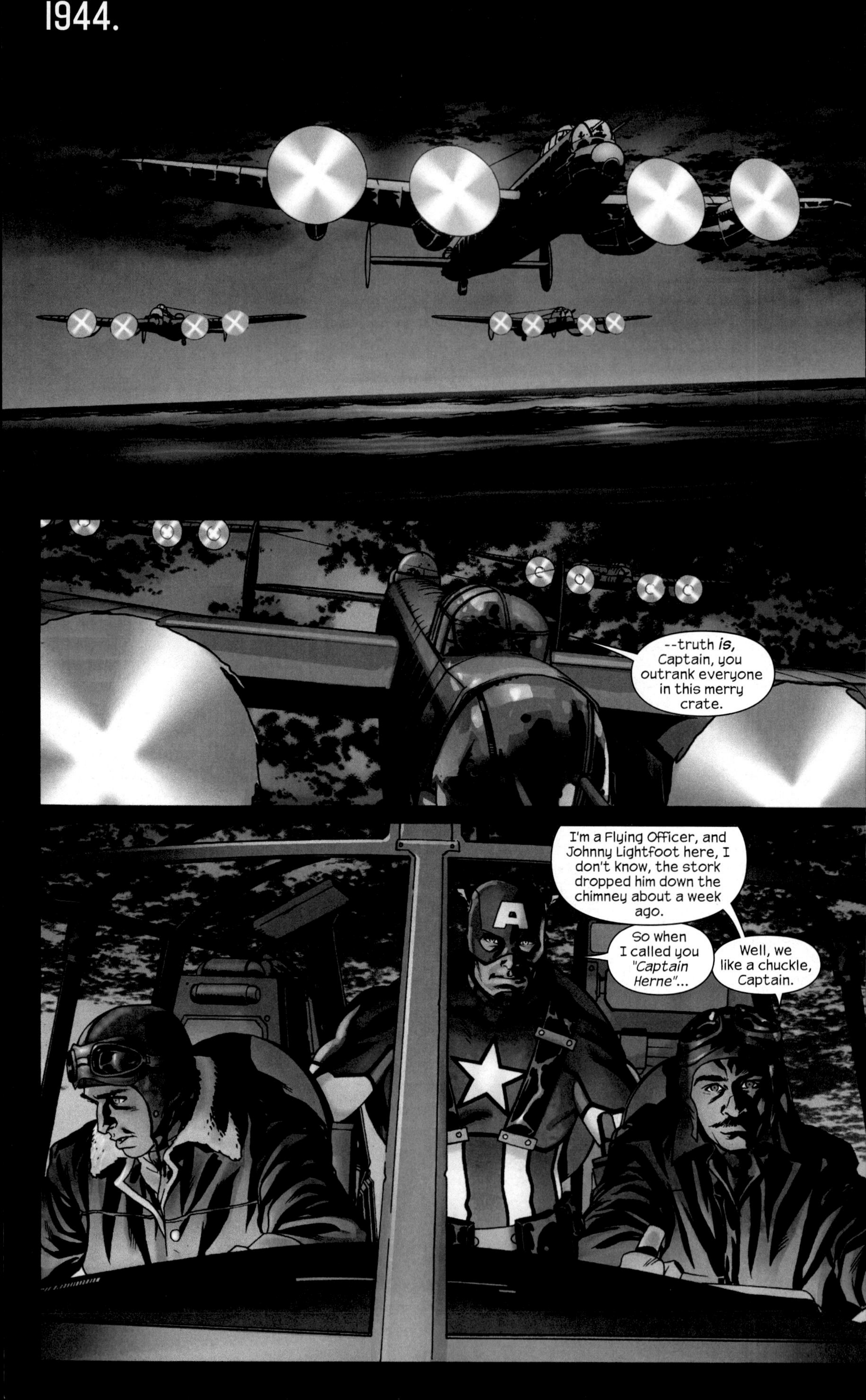
1944.
--truth *is,* Captain, you outrank everyone in this merry crate.
I'm a Flying Officer, and Johnny Lightfoot here, I don't know, the stork dropped him down the chimney about a week ago.
So when I called you *"Captain Herne"*...
Well, we like a chuckle, Captain.

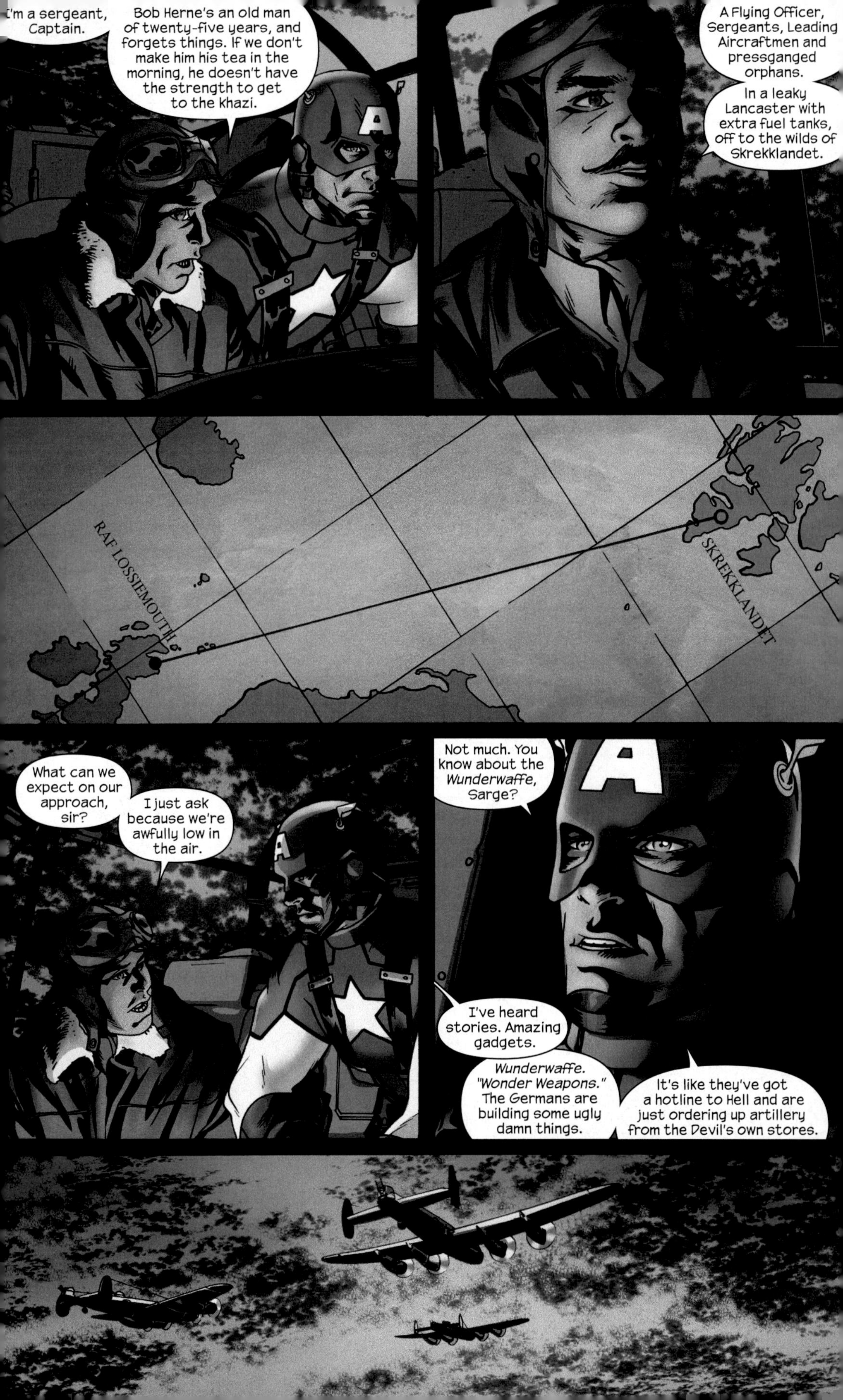

I'm a sergeant, Captain.
Bob Herne's an old man of twenty-five years, and forgets things. If we don't make him his tea in the morning, he doesn't have the strength to get to the khazi.
A Flying Officer, Sergeants, Leading Aircraftmen and pressganged orphans.
In a leaky Lancaster with extra fuel tanks, off to the wilds of Skrekklandet.
RAF LOSSIEMOUTH
SKREKKLANDET
What can we expect on our approach, sir?
I just ask because we're awfully low in the air.
Not much. You know about the *Wunderwaffe*, Sarge?
I've heard stories. Amazing gadgets.
Wunderwaffe. *"Wonder Weapons."* The Germans are building some ugly damn things.
It's like they've got a hotline to Hell and are just ordering up artillery from the Devil's own stores.

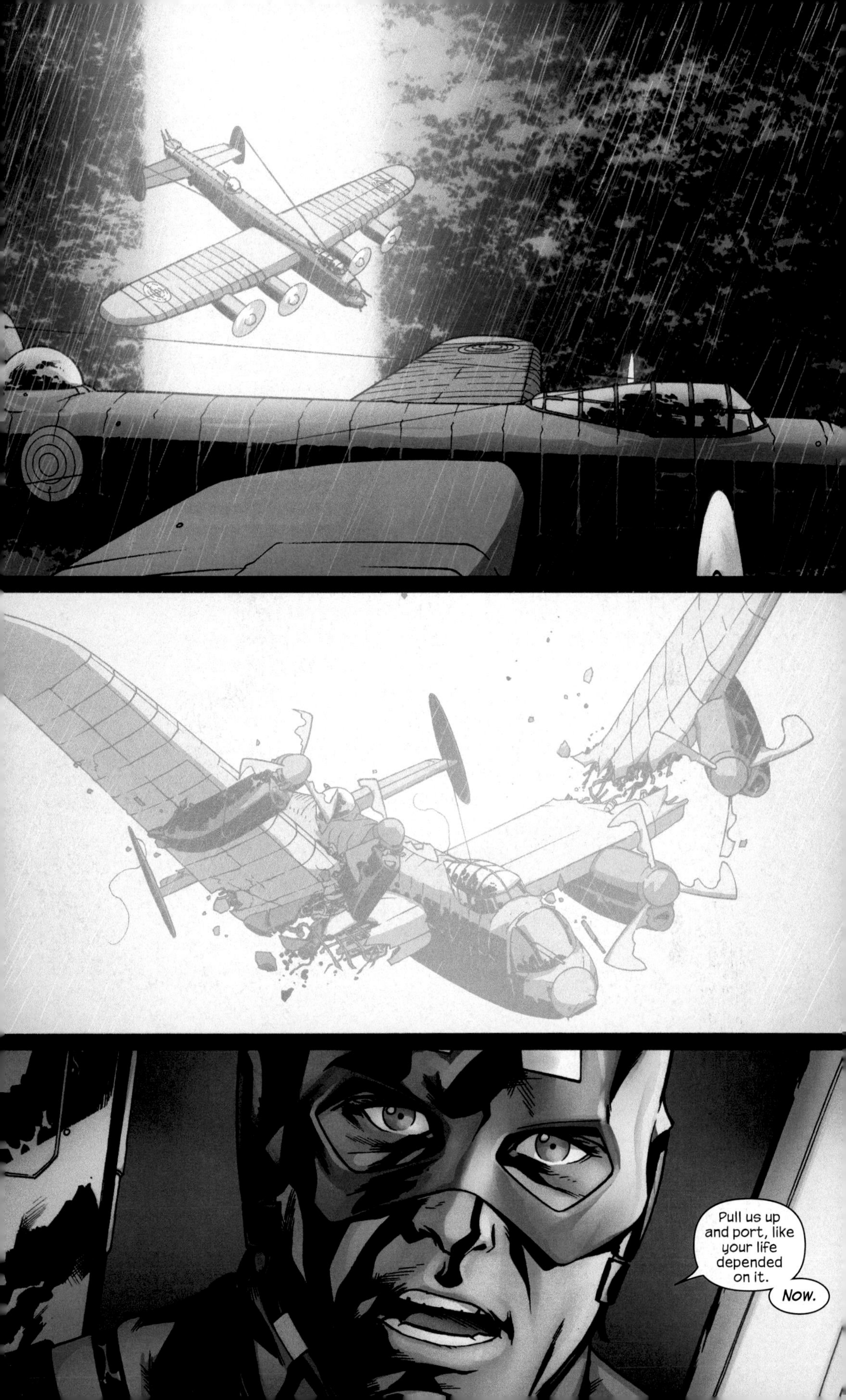
Pull us up and port, like your life depended on it.
NOW.

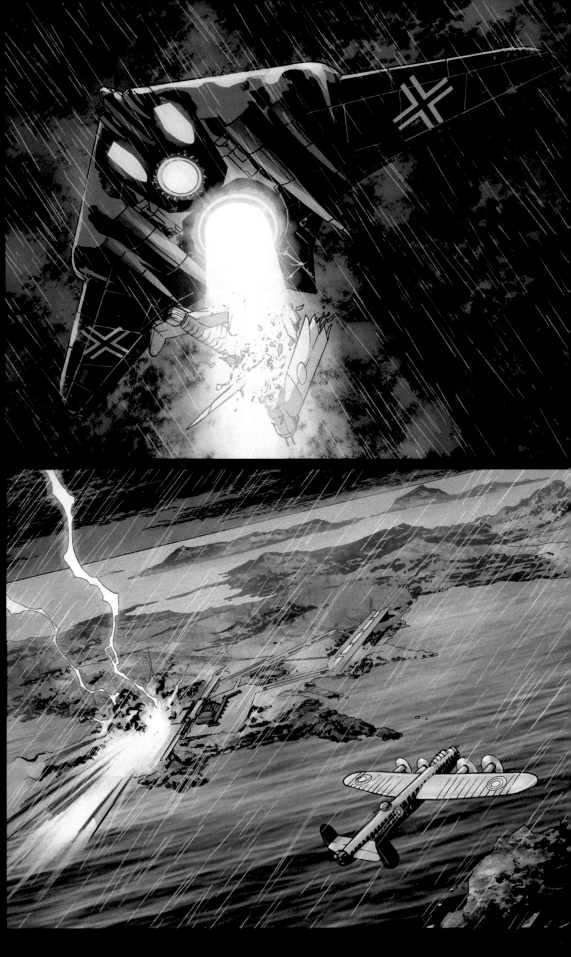

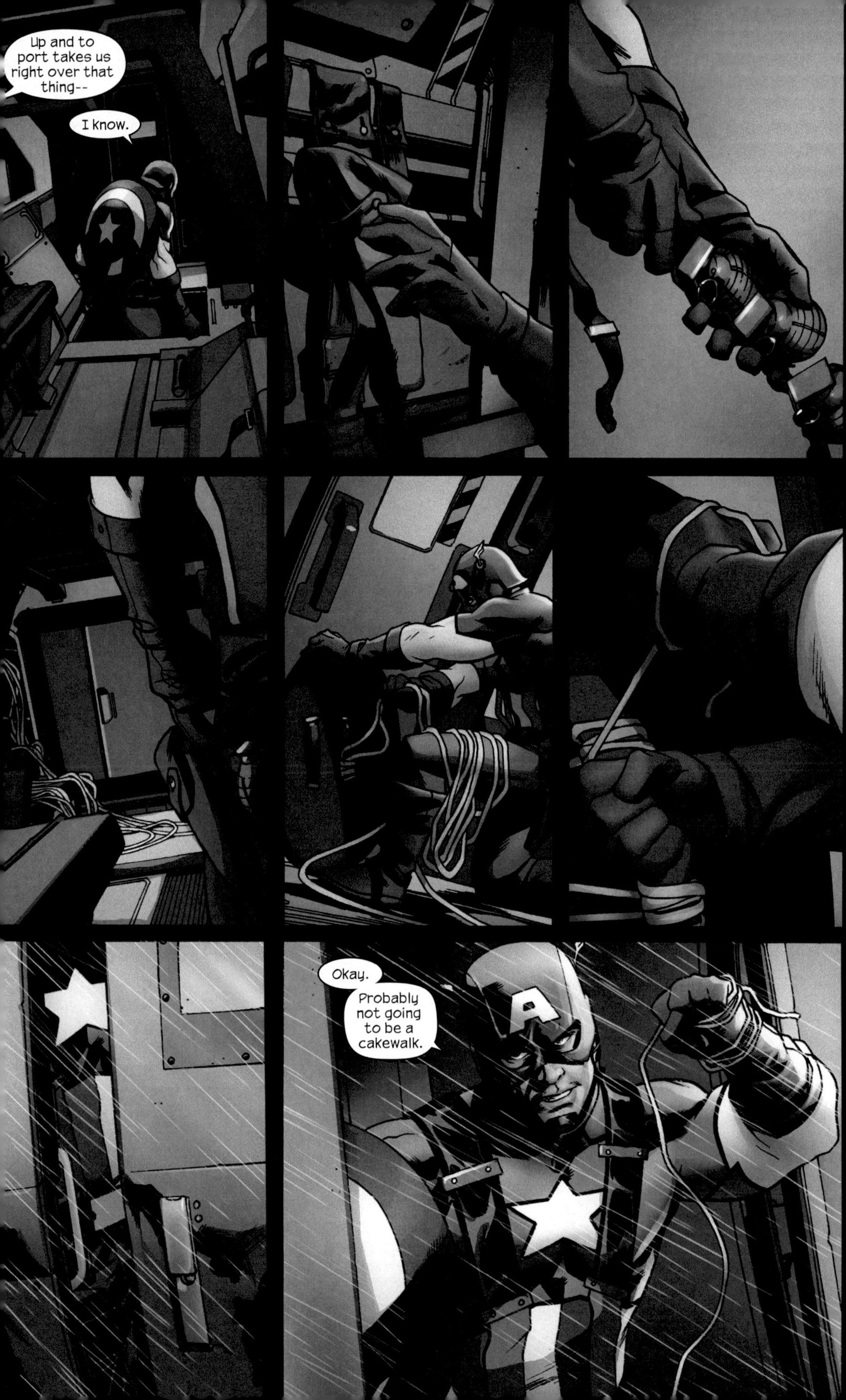
Up and to port takes us right over that thing--
I know.
Okay.
Probably not going to be a cakewalk.

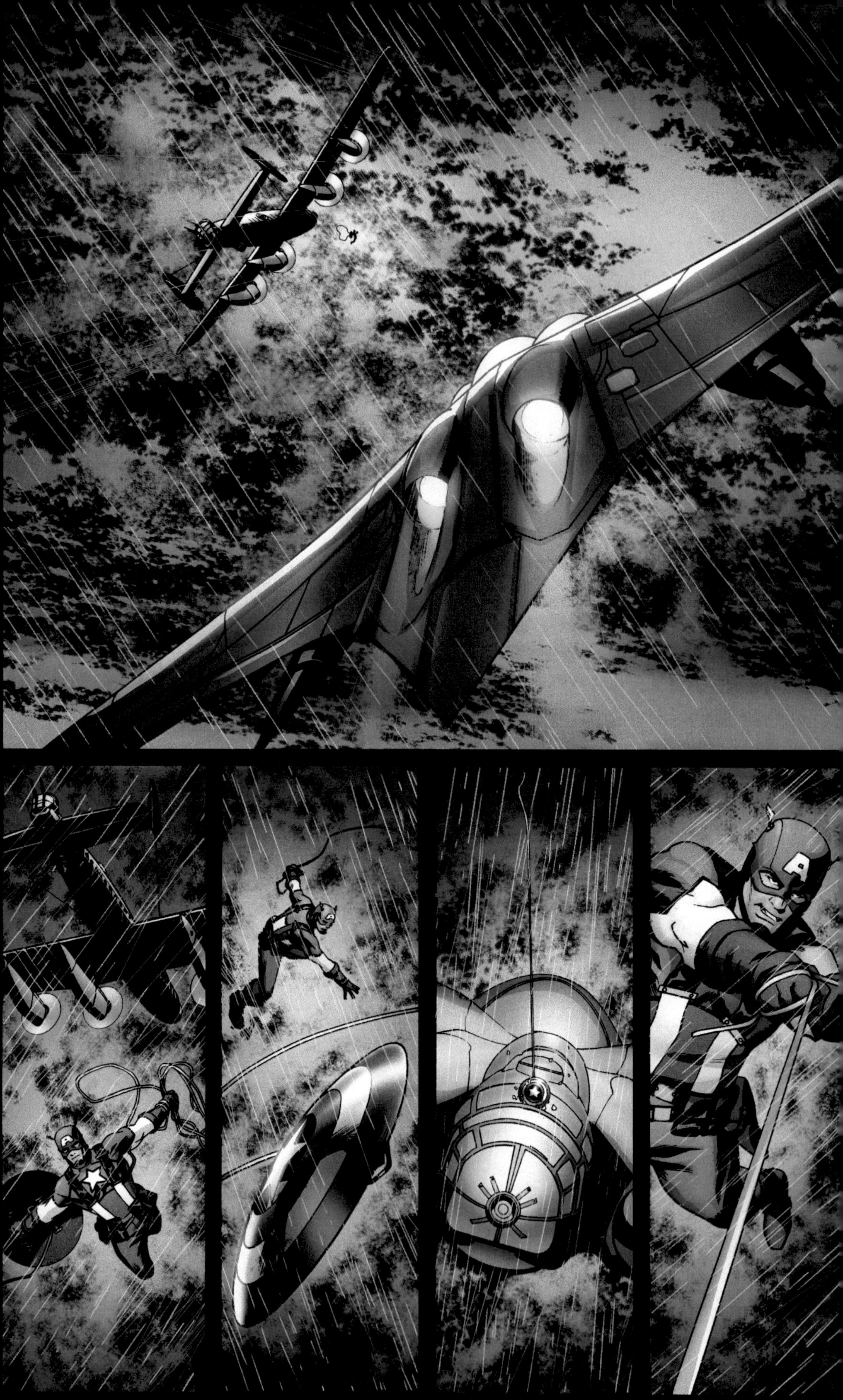

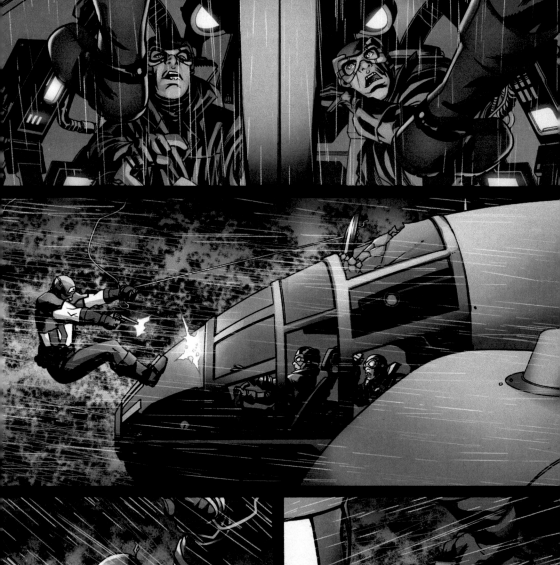

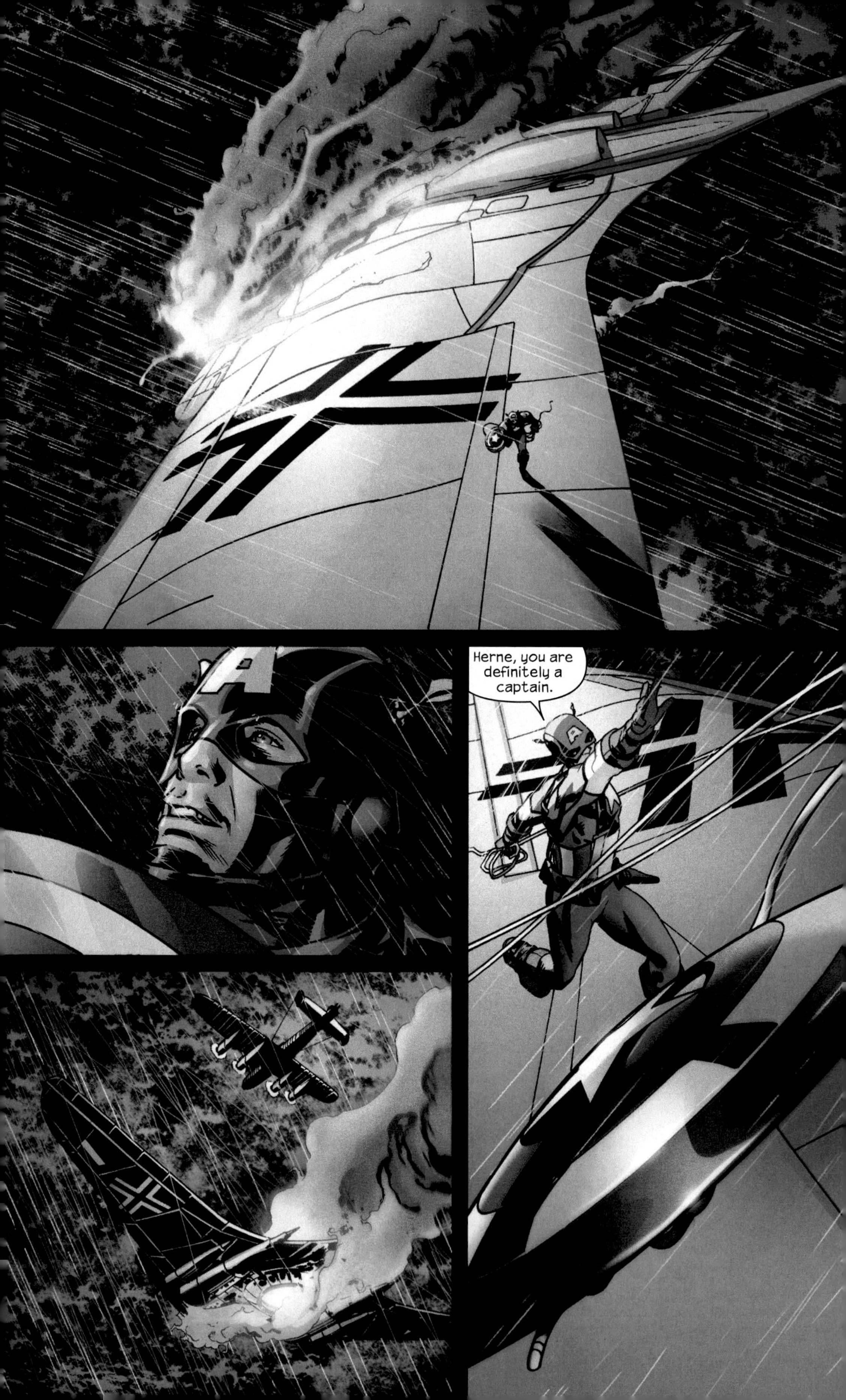
Herne, you are definitely a captain.

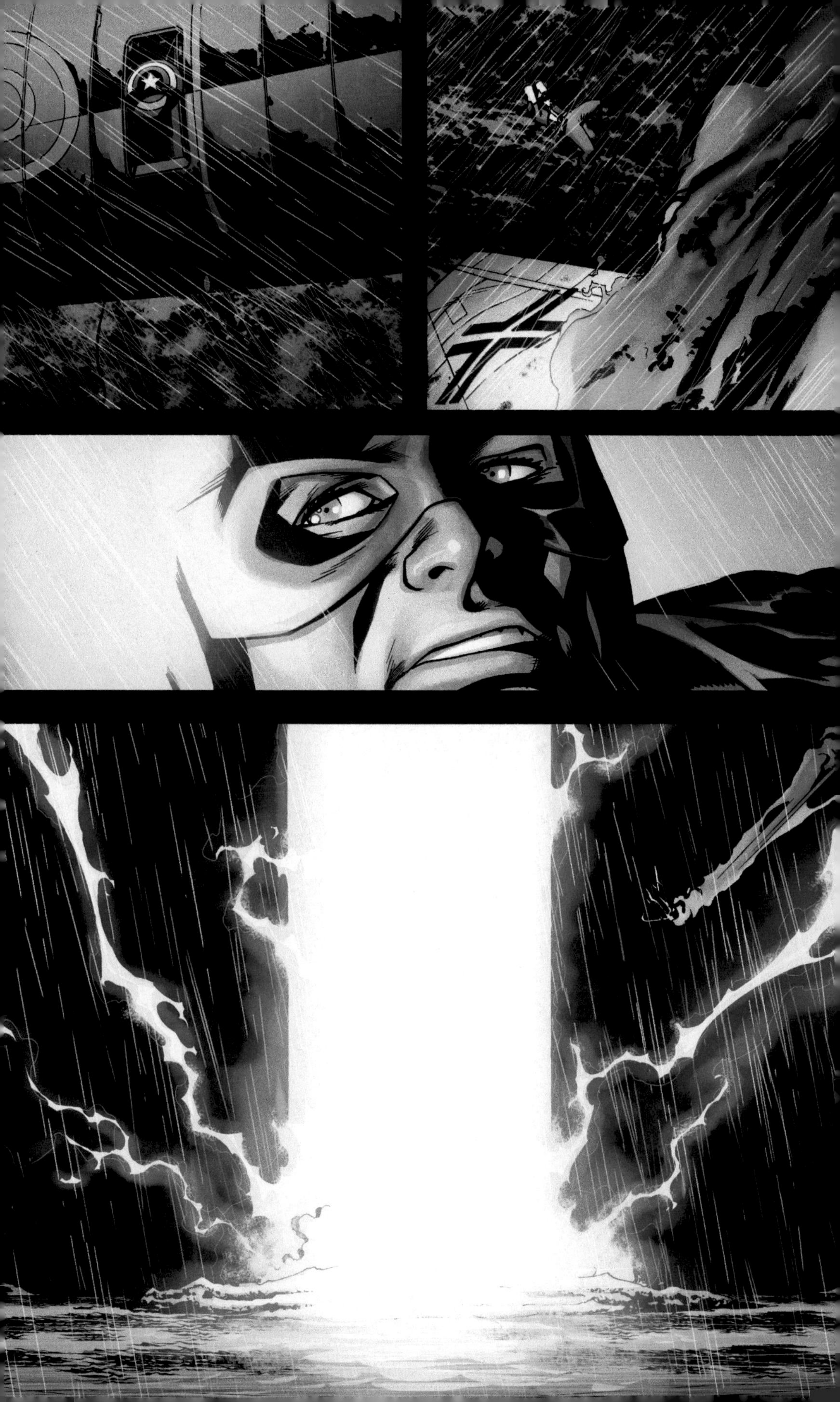

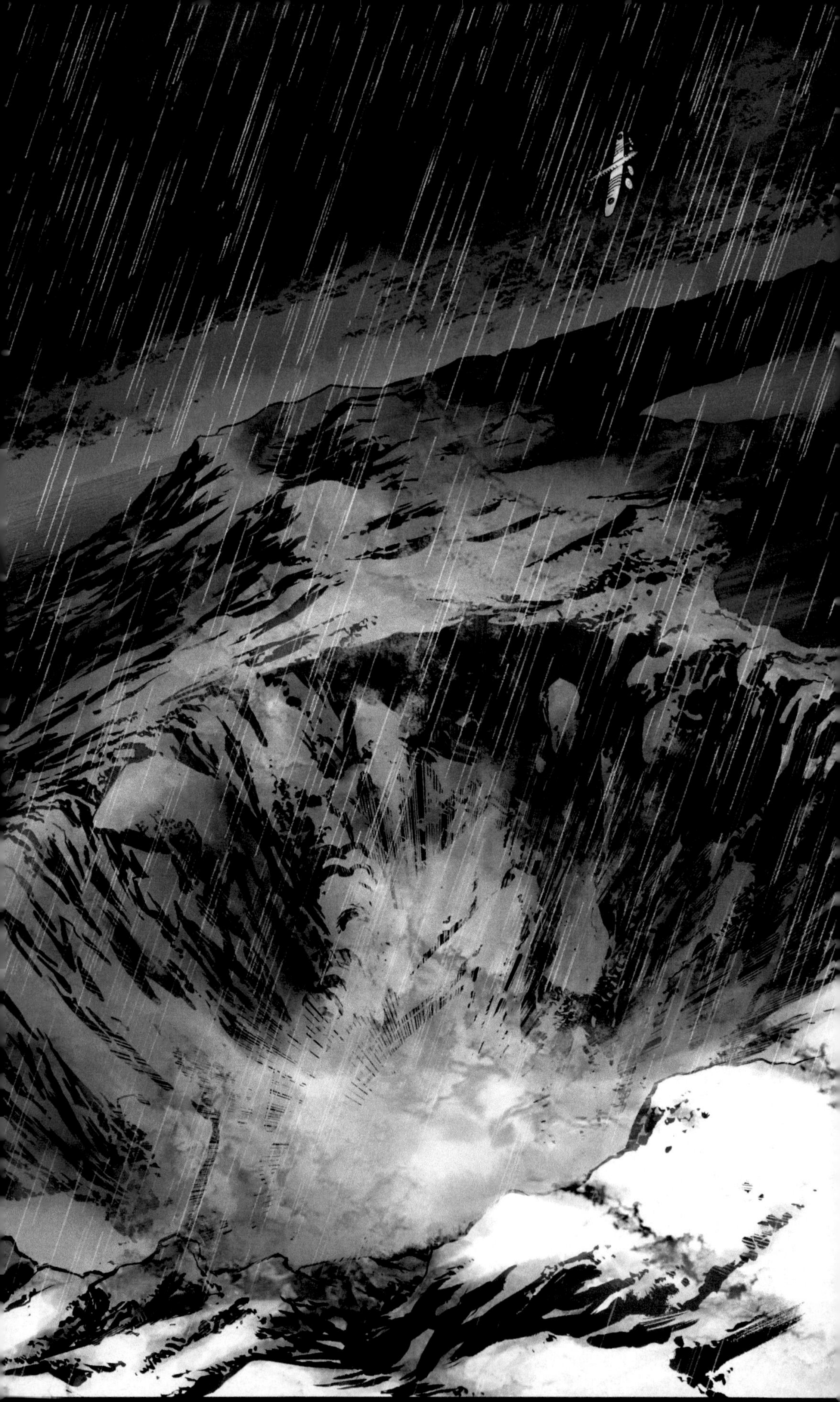

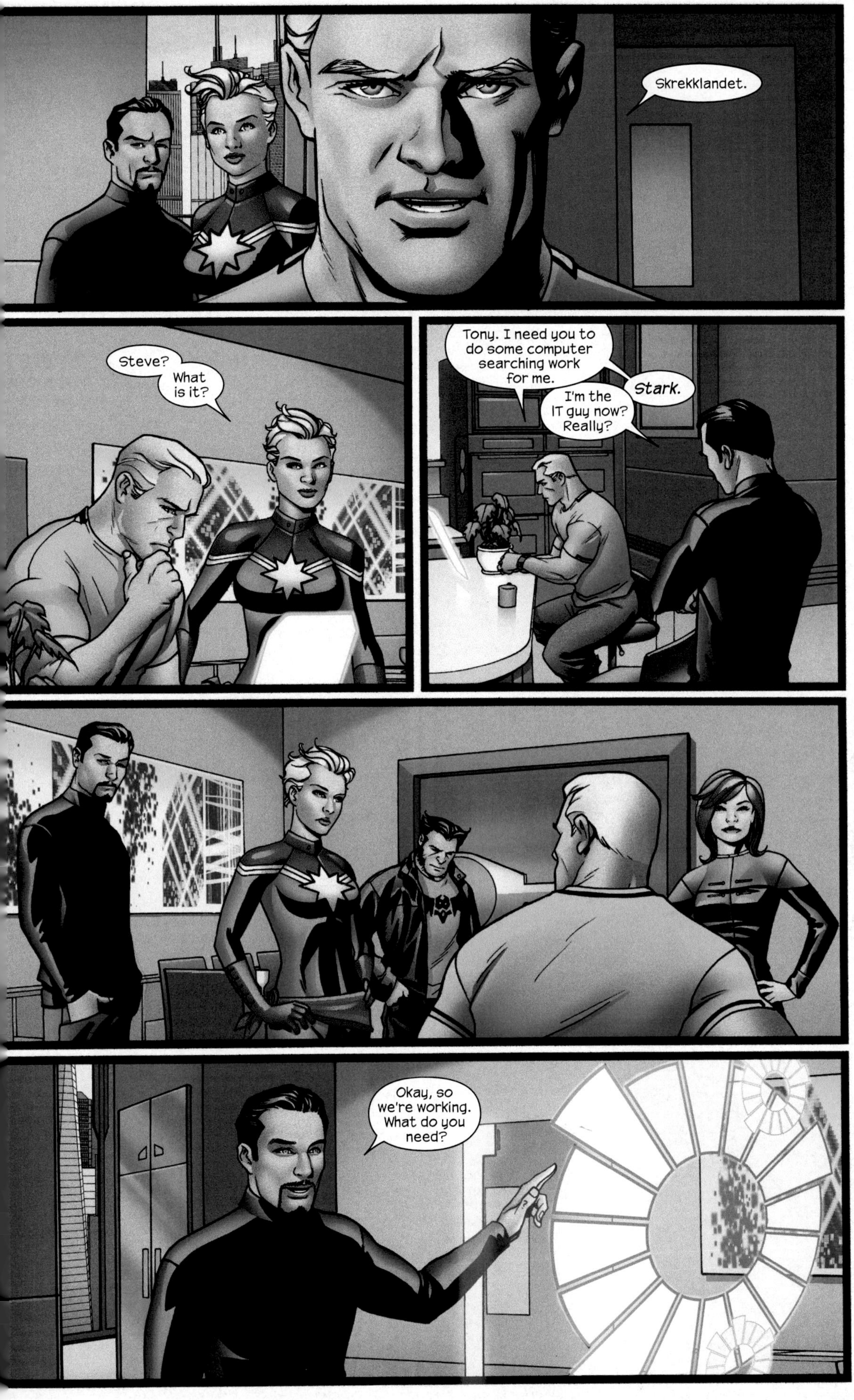
Skrekklandet.
Steve? What is it?
Tony. I need you to do some computer searching work for me.
Stark.
I'm the IT guy now? Really?
Okay, so we're working. What do you need?

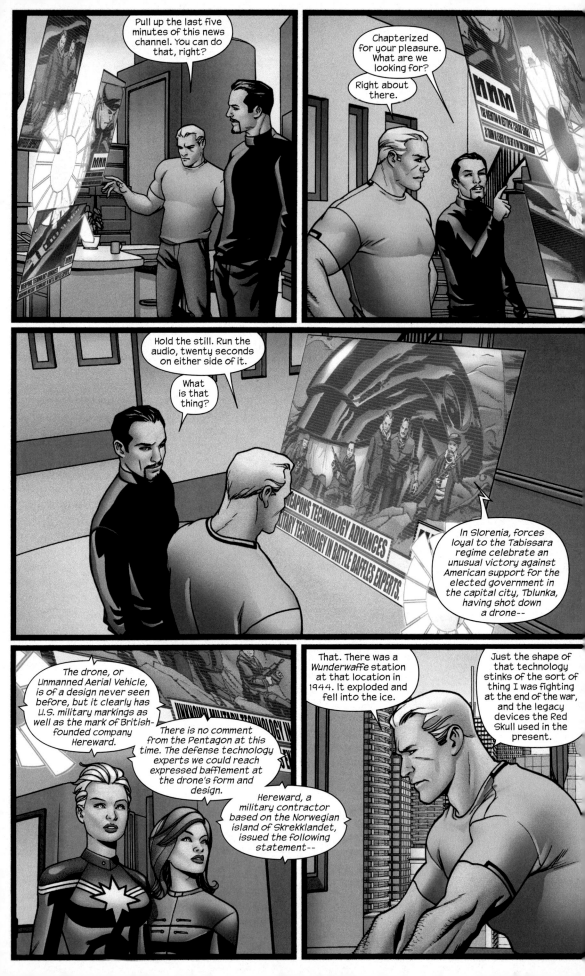

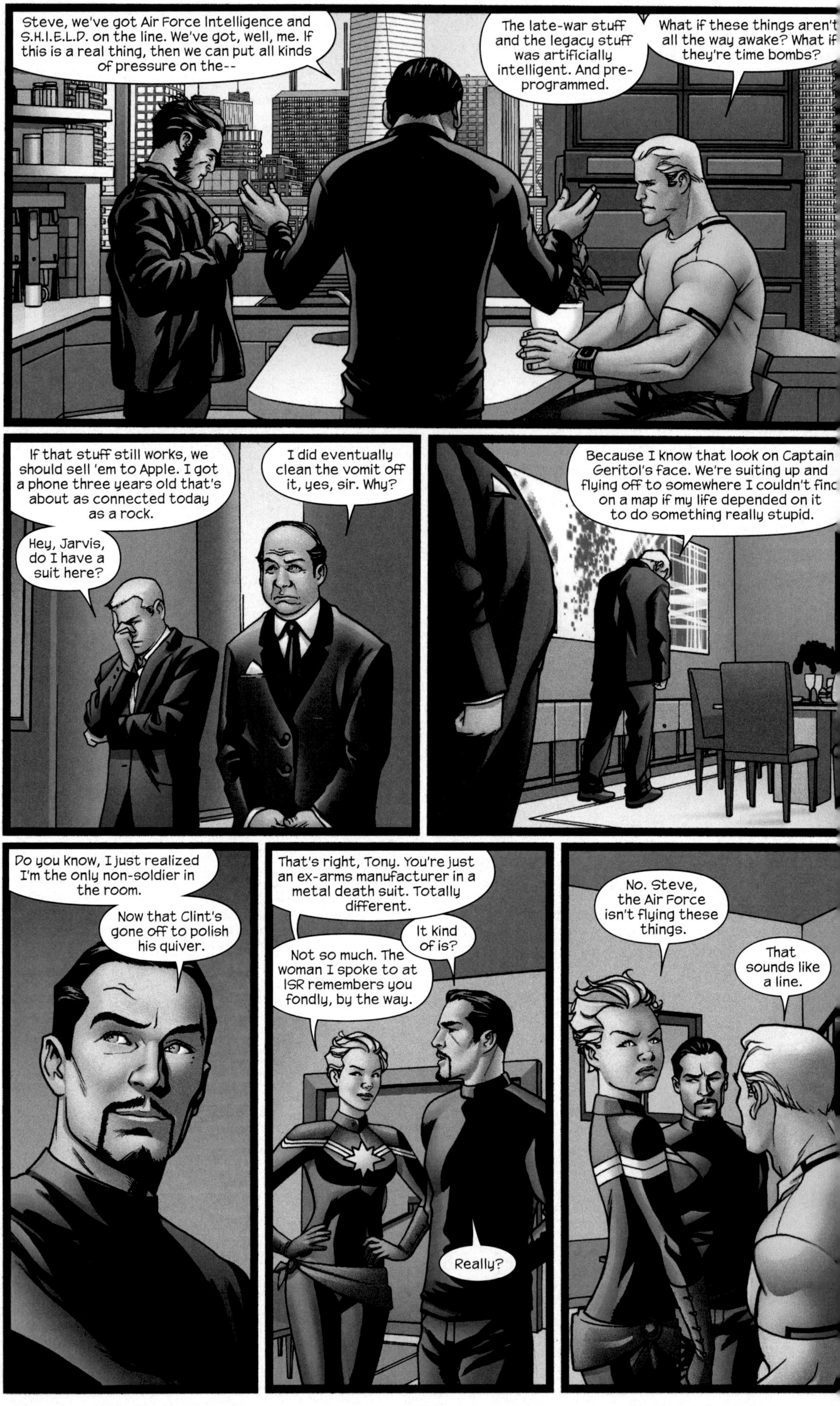

Steve, we've got Air Force Intelligence and S.H.I.E.L.D. on the line. We've got, well, me. If this is a real thing, then we can put all kinds of pressure on the--
The late-war stuff and the legacy stuff was artificially intelligent. And pre-programmed.
What if these things aren't all the way awake? What if they're time bombs?
If that stuff still works, we should sell 'em to Apple. I got a phone three years old that's about as connected today as a rock.
Hey, Jarvis, do I have a suit here?
I did eventually clean the vomit off it, yes, sir. Why?
Because I know that look on Captain Geritol's face. We're suiting up and flying off to somewhere I couldn't find on a map if my life depended on it to do something really stupid.
Do you know, I just realized I'm the only non-soldier in the room.
Now that Clint's gone off to polish his quiver.
That's right, Tony. You're just an ex-arms manufacturer in a metal death suit. Totally different.
It kind of is?
Not so much. The woman I spoke to at ISR remembers you fondly, by the way.
Really?
No. Steve, the Air Force isn't flying these things.
That sounds like a line.

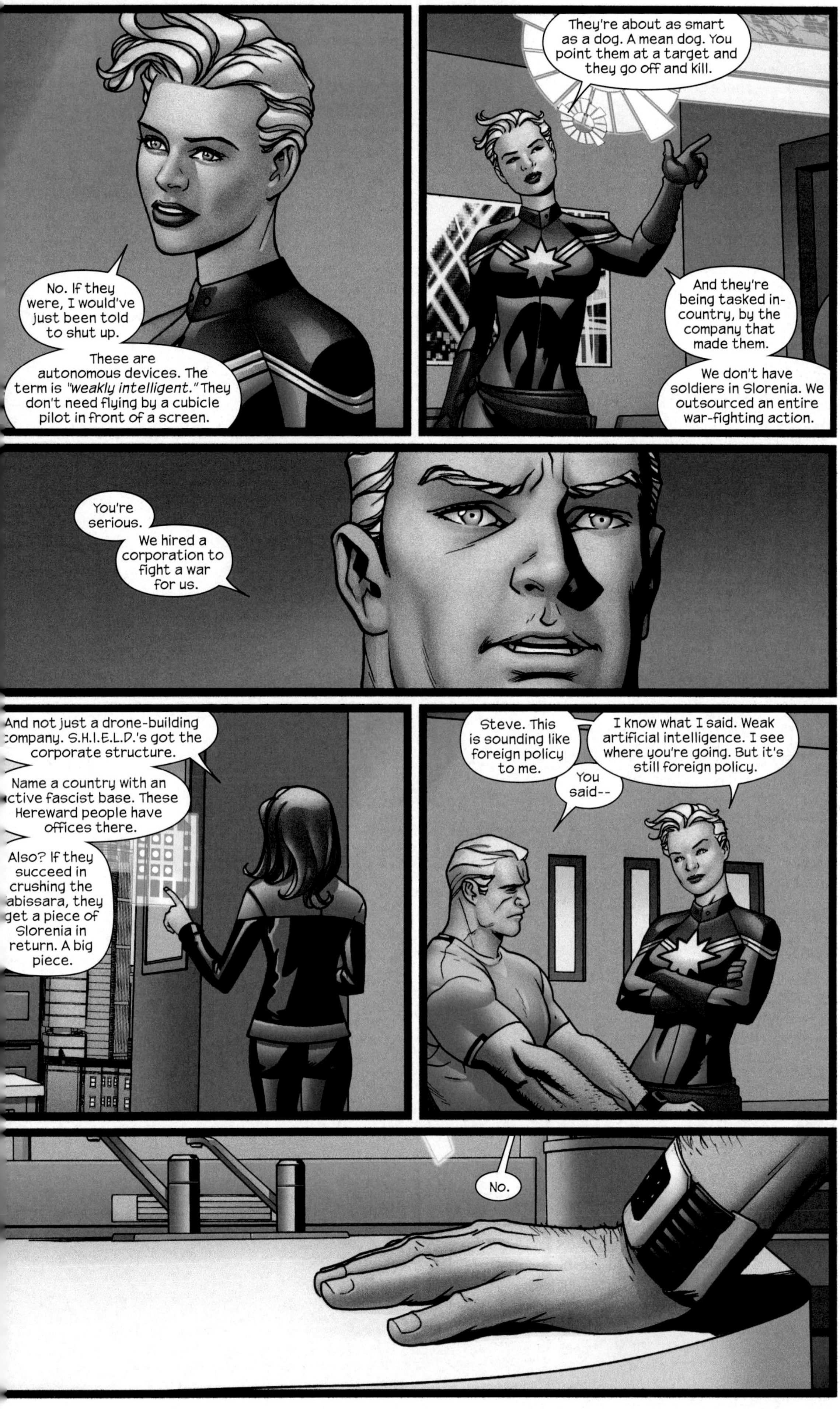

No. If they were, I would've just been told to shut up.
These are autonomous devices. The term is *"weakly intelligent."* They don't need flying by a cubicle pilot in front of a screen.
They're about as smart as a dog. A mean dog. You point them at a target and they go off and kill.
And they're being tasked in-country, by the company that made them.
We don't have soldiers in Slorenia. We outsourced an entire war-fighting action.
You're serious.
We hired a corporation to fight a war for us.
And not just a drone-building company. S.H.I.E.L.D.'s got the corporate structure.
Name a country with an active fascist base. These Hereward people have offices there.
Also? If they succeed in crushing the Abissara, they get a piece of Slorenia in return. A big piece.
Steve. This is sounding like foreign policy to me.
You said--
I know what I said. Weak artificial intelligence. I see where you're going. But it's still foreign policy.
No.

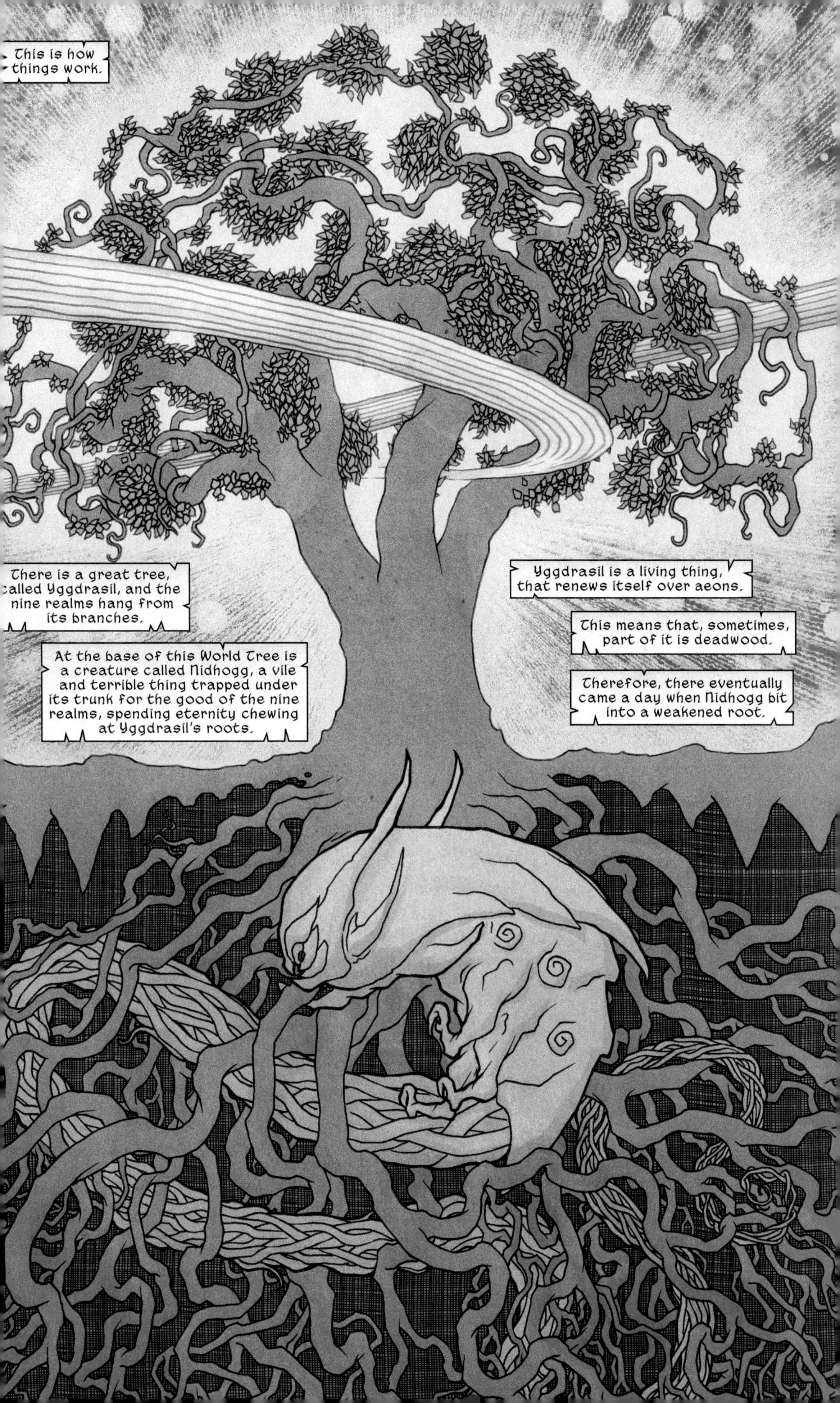

This is how things work.
There is a great tree, called Yggdrasil, and the nine realms hang from its branches.
At the base of this World Tree is a creature called Nidhogg, a vile and terrible thing trapped under its trunk for the good of the nine realms, spending eternity chewing at Yggdrasil's roots.
Yggdrasil is a living thing, that renews itself over aeons.
This means that, sometimes, part of it is deadwood.
Therefore, there eventually came a day when Nidhogg bit into a weakened root.

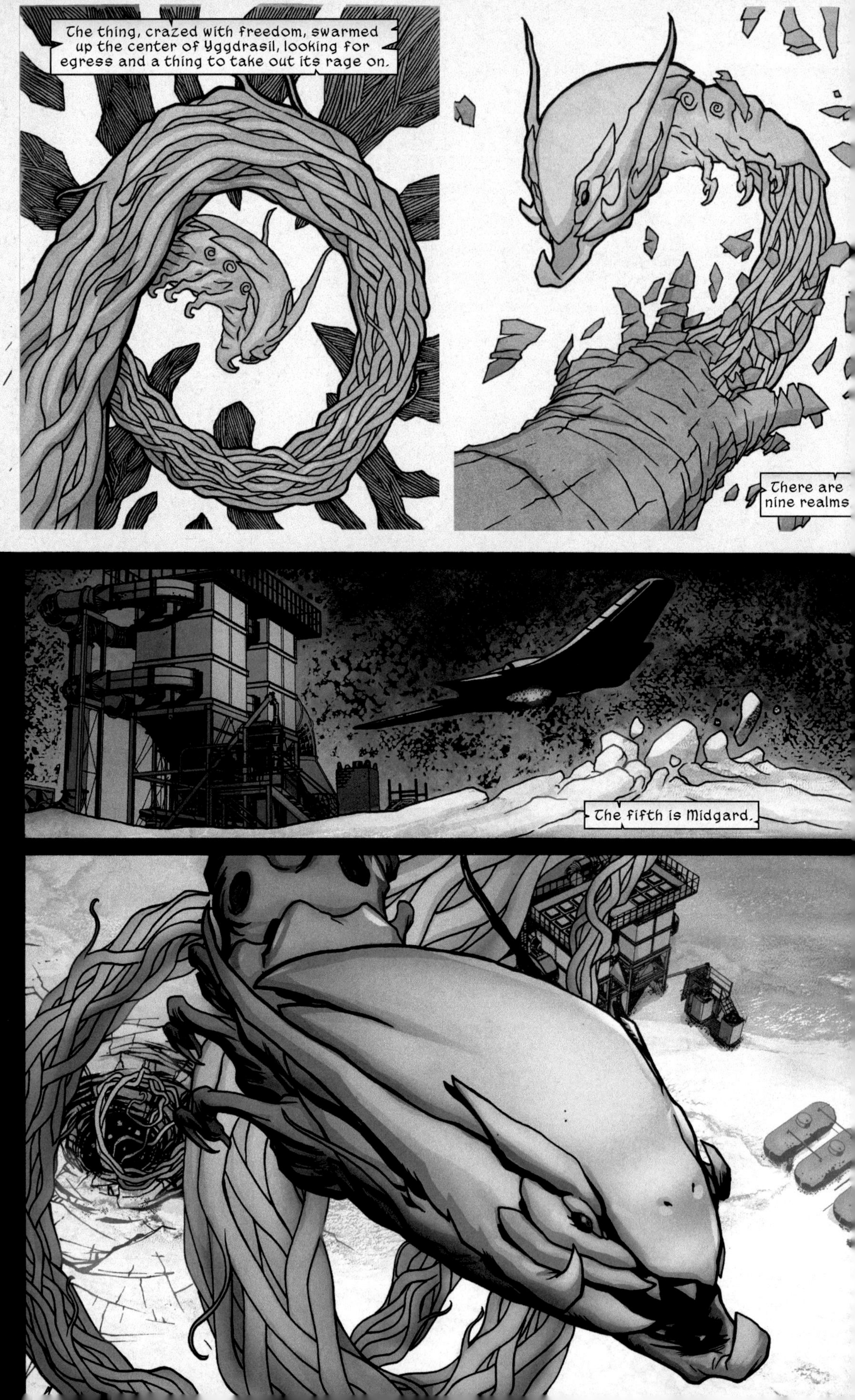
The thing, crazed with freedom, swarmed up the center of Yggdrasil, looking for egress and a thing to take out its rage on.
There are nine realms
The fifth is Midgard.

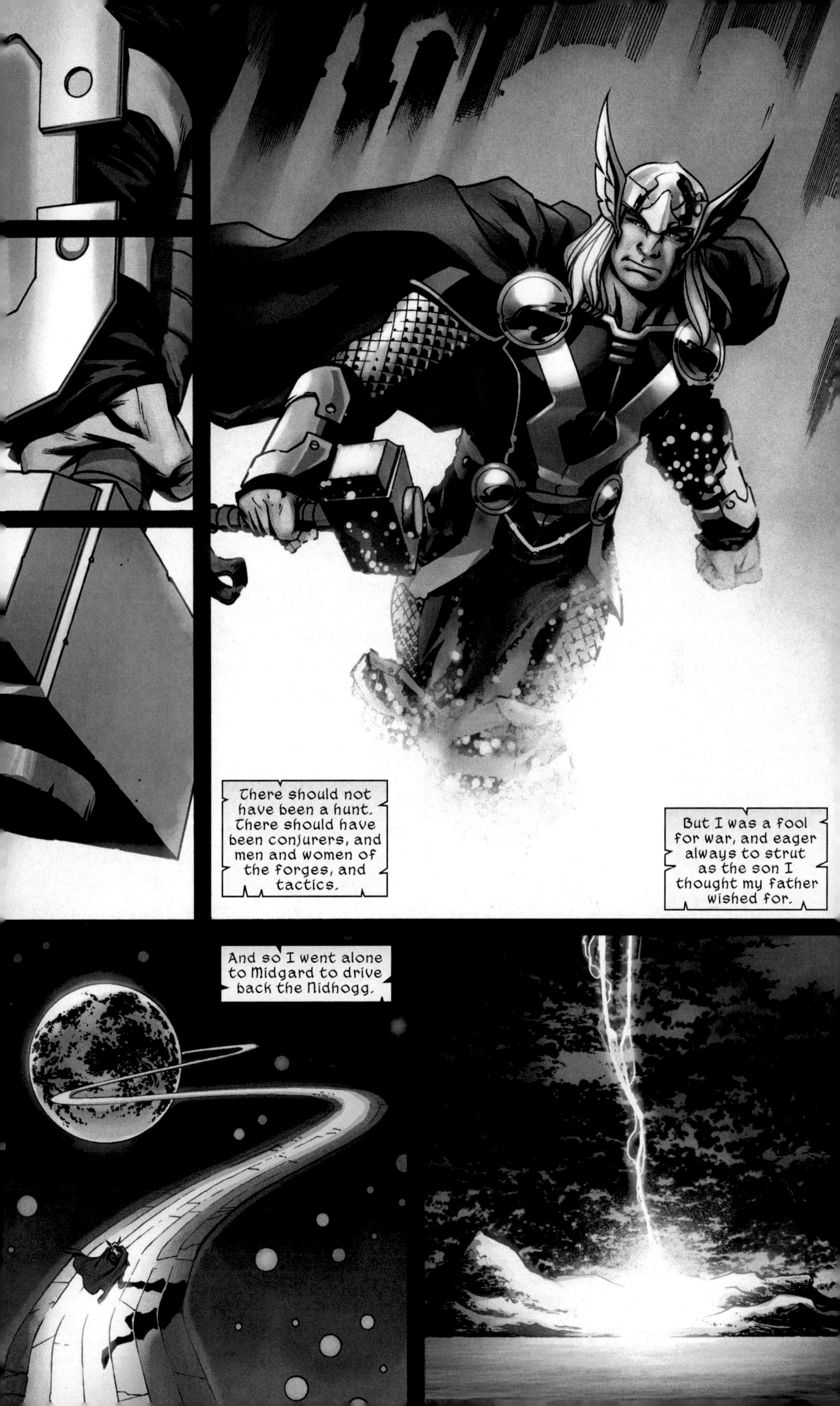
There should not have been a hunt. There should have been conjurers, and men and women of the forges, and tactics.
But I was a fool for war, and eager always to strut as the son I thought my father wished for.
And so I went alone to Midgard to drive back the Nidhogg.

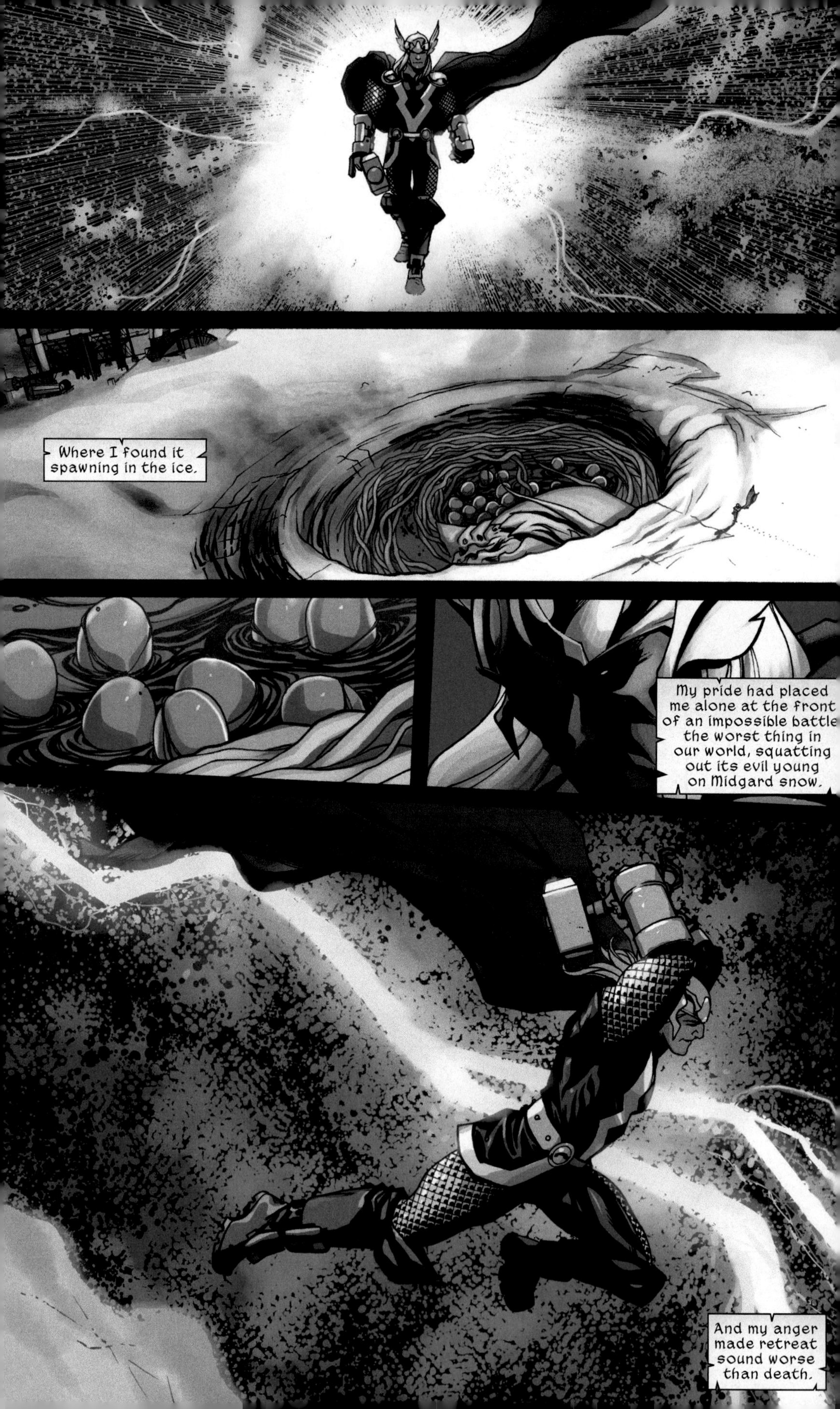
Where I found it spawning in the ice.
My pride had placed me alone at the front of an impossible battle the worst thing in our world, squatting out its evil young on Midgard snow.
And my anger made retreat sound worse than death.

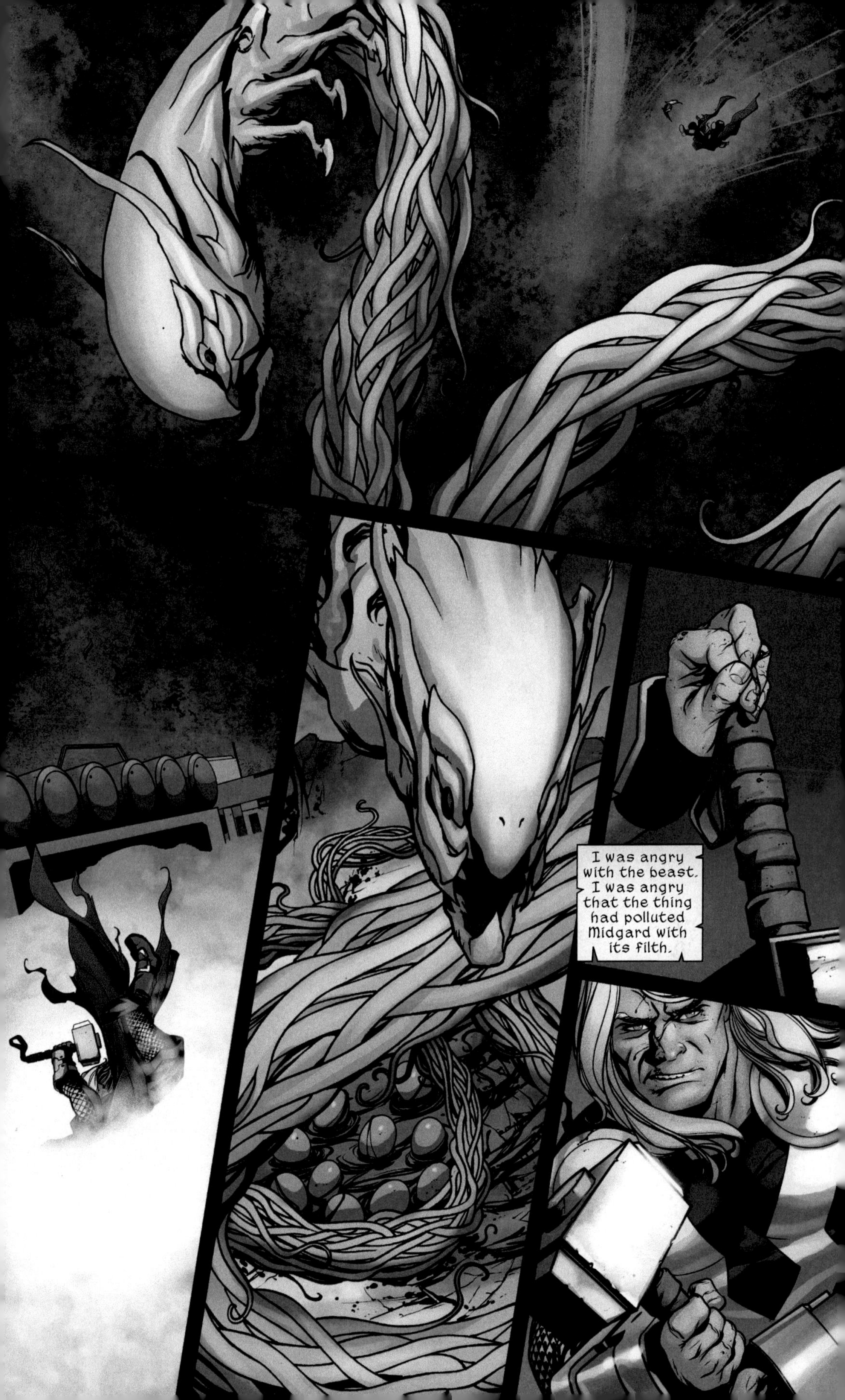
I was angry with the beast. I was angry that the thing had polluted Midgard with its filth.

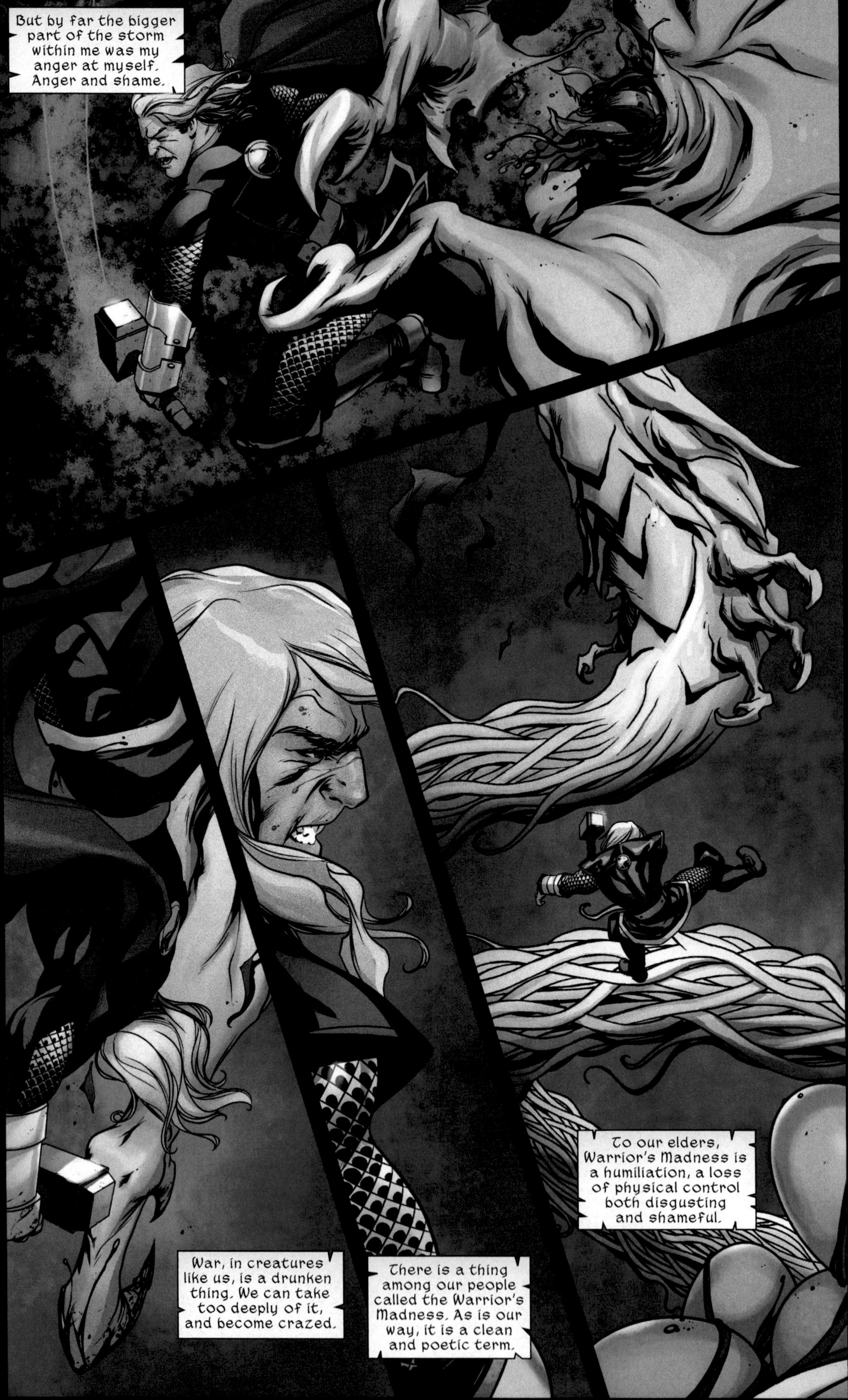
But by far the bigger part of the storm within me was my anger at myself. Anger and shame.
War, in creatures like us, is a drunken thing. We can take too deeply of it, and become crazed.
There is a thing among our people called the Warrior's Madness. As is our way, it is a clean and poetic term.
To our elders, Warrior's Madness is a humiliation, a loss of physical control both disgusting and shameful.

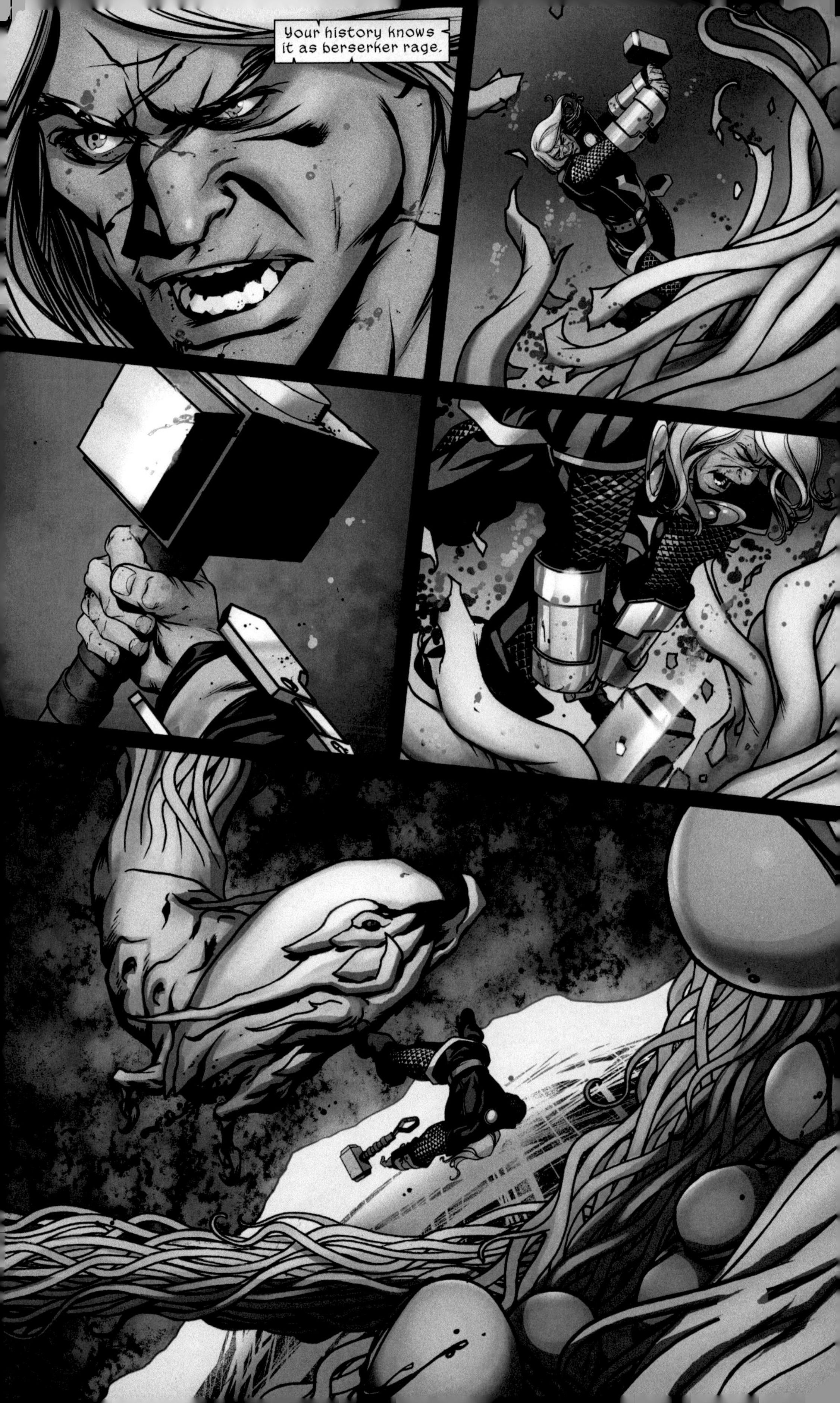
Your history knows
it as berserker rage.

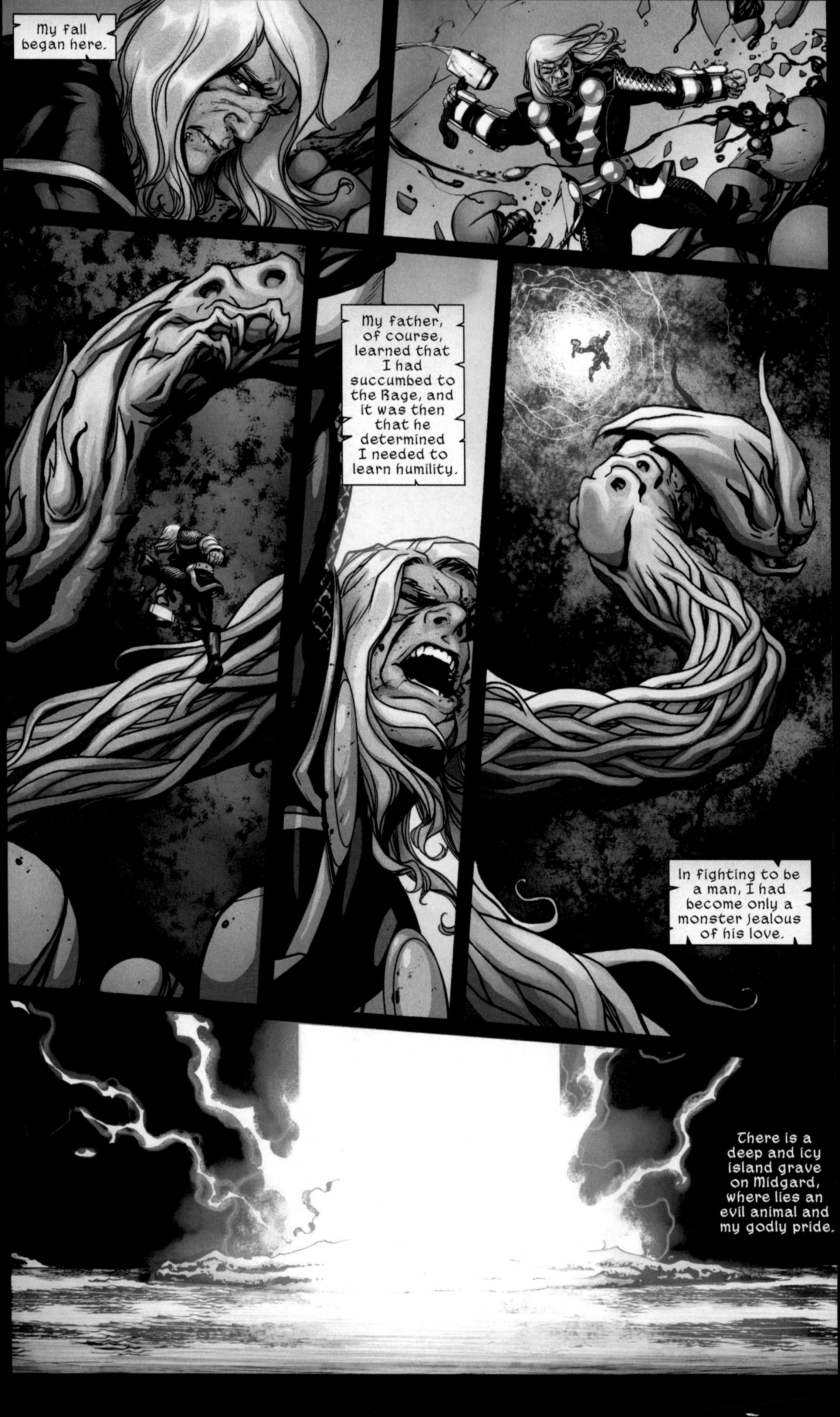
My fall began here.
My father, of course, learned that I had succumbed to the Rage, and it was then that he determined I needed to learn humility.
In fighting to be a man, I had become only a monster jealous of his love.
There is a deep and icy island grave on Midgard, where lies an evil animal and my godly pride.

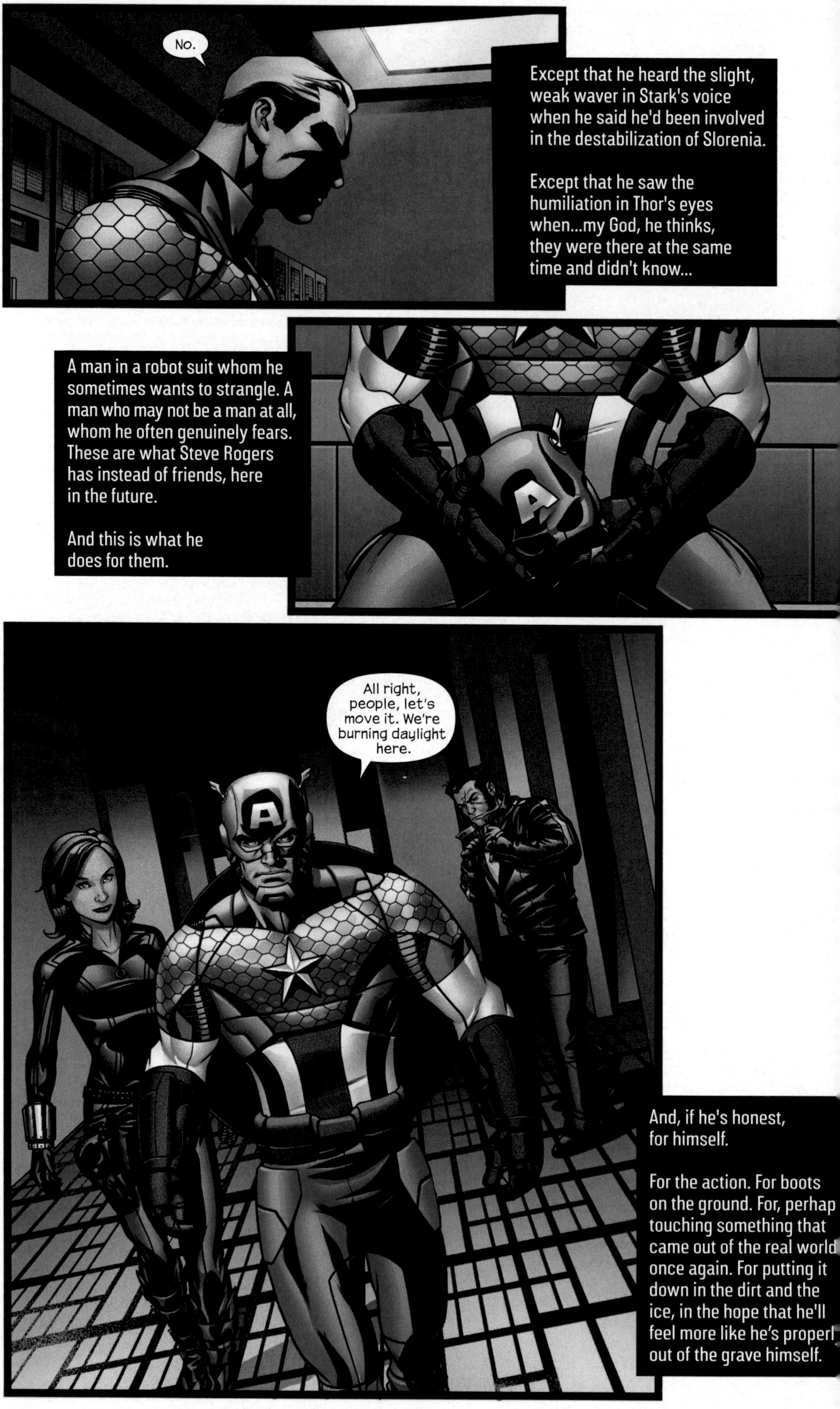
No.
Except that he heard the slight, weak waver in Stark's voice when he said he'd been involved in the destabilization of Slorenia.
Except that he saw the humiliation in Thor's eyes when...my God, he thinks, they were there at the same time and didn't know...
A man in a robot suit whom he sometimes wants to strangle. A man who may not be a man at all, whom he often genuinely fears. These are what Steve Rogers has instead of friends, here in the future.
And this is what he does for them.
All right, people, let's move it. We're burning daylight here.
And, if he's honest, for himself.
For the action. For boots on the ground. For, perhap touching something that came out of the real world once again. For putting it down in the dirt and the ice, in the hope that he'll feel more like he's properl out of the grave himself.

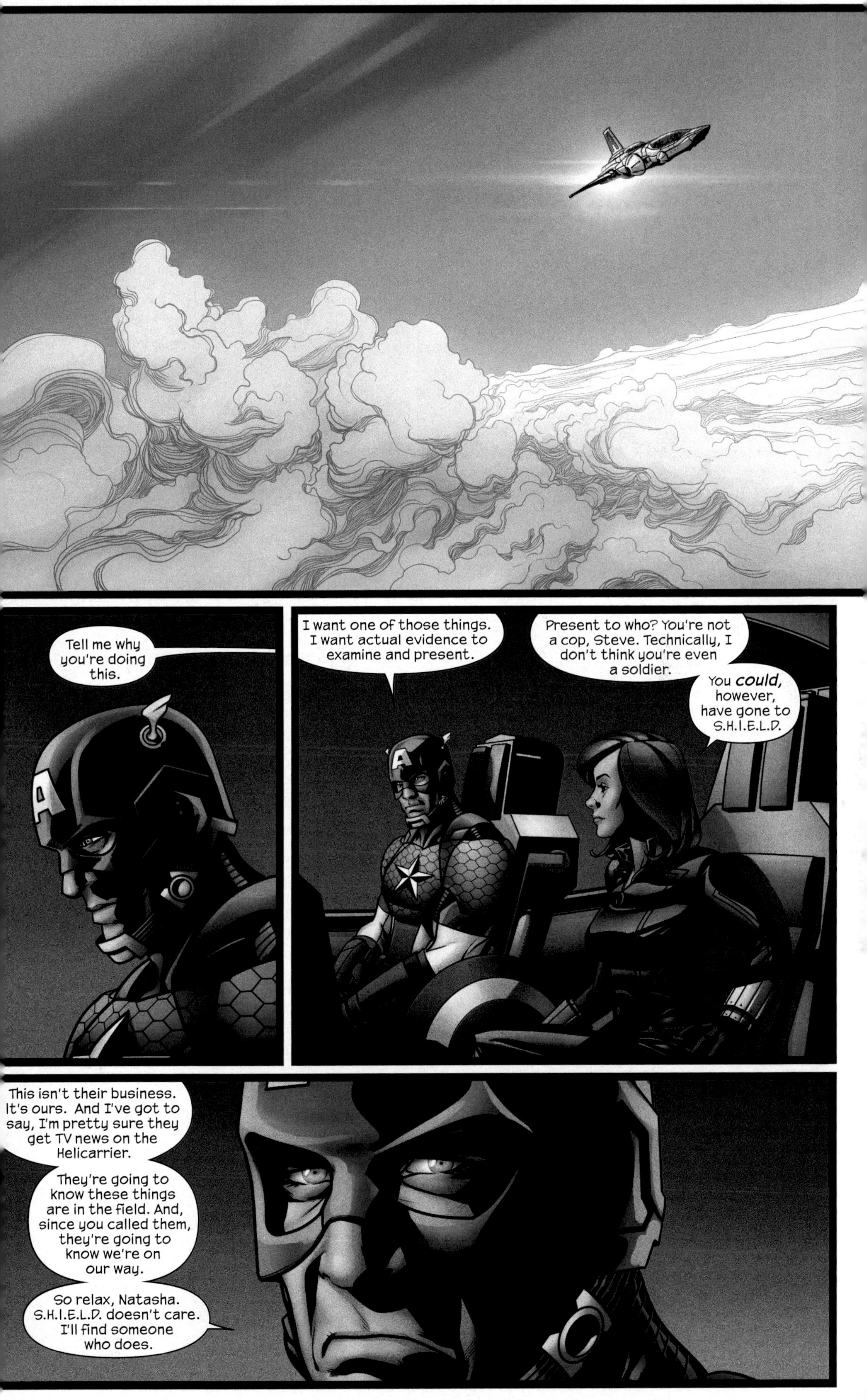

Tell me why you're doing this.
I want one of those things. I want actual evidence to examine and present.
Present to who? You're not a cop, Steve. Technically, I don't think you're even a soldier.
You **could,** however, have gone to S.H.I.E.L.D.
This isn't their business. It's ours. And I've got to say, I'm pretty sure they get TV news on the Helicarrier.
They're going to know these things are in the field. And, since you called them, they're going to know we're on our way.
So relax, Natasha. S.H.I.E.L.D. doesn't care. I'll find someone who does.

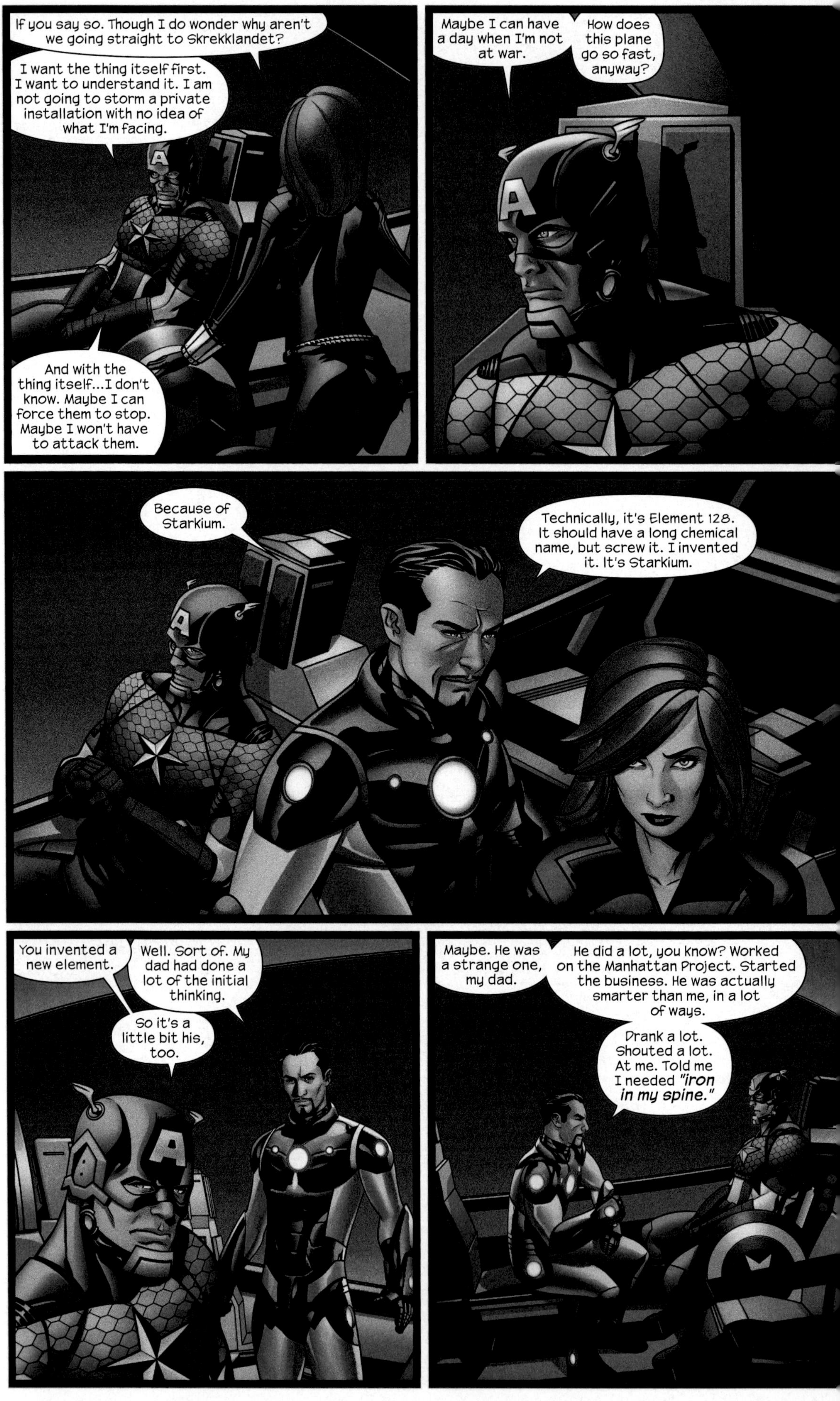
If you say so. Though I do wonder why aren't we going straight to Skrekklandet?
I want the thing itself first. I want to understand it. I am not going to storm a private installation with no idea of what I'm facing.
And with the thing itself...I don't know. Maybe I can force them to stop. Maybe I won't have to attack them.
Maybe I can have a day when I'm not at war.
How does this plane go so fast, anyway?
Because of Starkium.
Technically, it's Element 128. It should have a long chemical name, but screw it. I invented it. It's Starkium.
You invented a new element.
Well. Sort of. My dad had done a lot of the initial thinking.
So it's a little bit his, too.
Maybe. He was a strange one, my dad.
He did a lot, you know? Worked on the Manhattan Project. Started the business. He was actually smarter than me, in a lot of ways.
Drank a lot. Shouted a lot. At me. Told me I needed *"iron in my spine."*

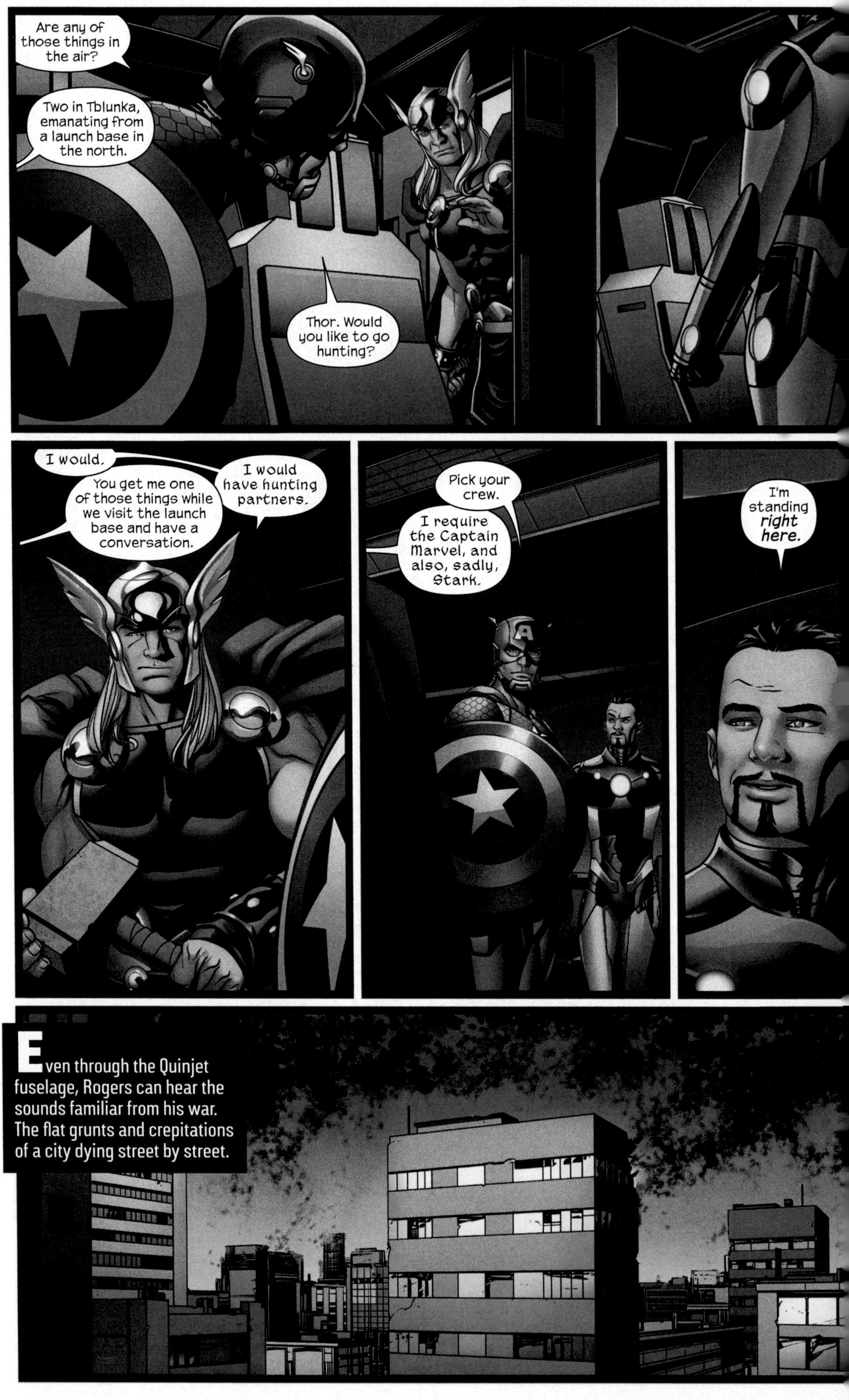
Are any of those things in the air?
Two in Tblunka, emanating from a launch base in the north.
Thor. Would you like to go hunting?
I would.
You get me one of those things while we visit the launch base and have a conversation.
I would have hunting partners.
Pick your crew.
I require the Captain Marvel, and also, sadly, Stark.
I'm standing *right here.*
Even through the Quinjet fuselage, Rogers can hear the sounds familiar from his war. The flat grunts and crepitations of a city dying street by street.

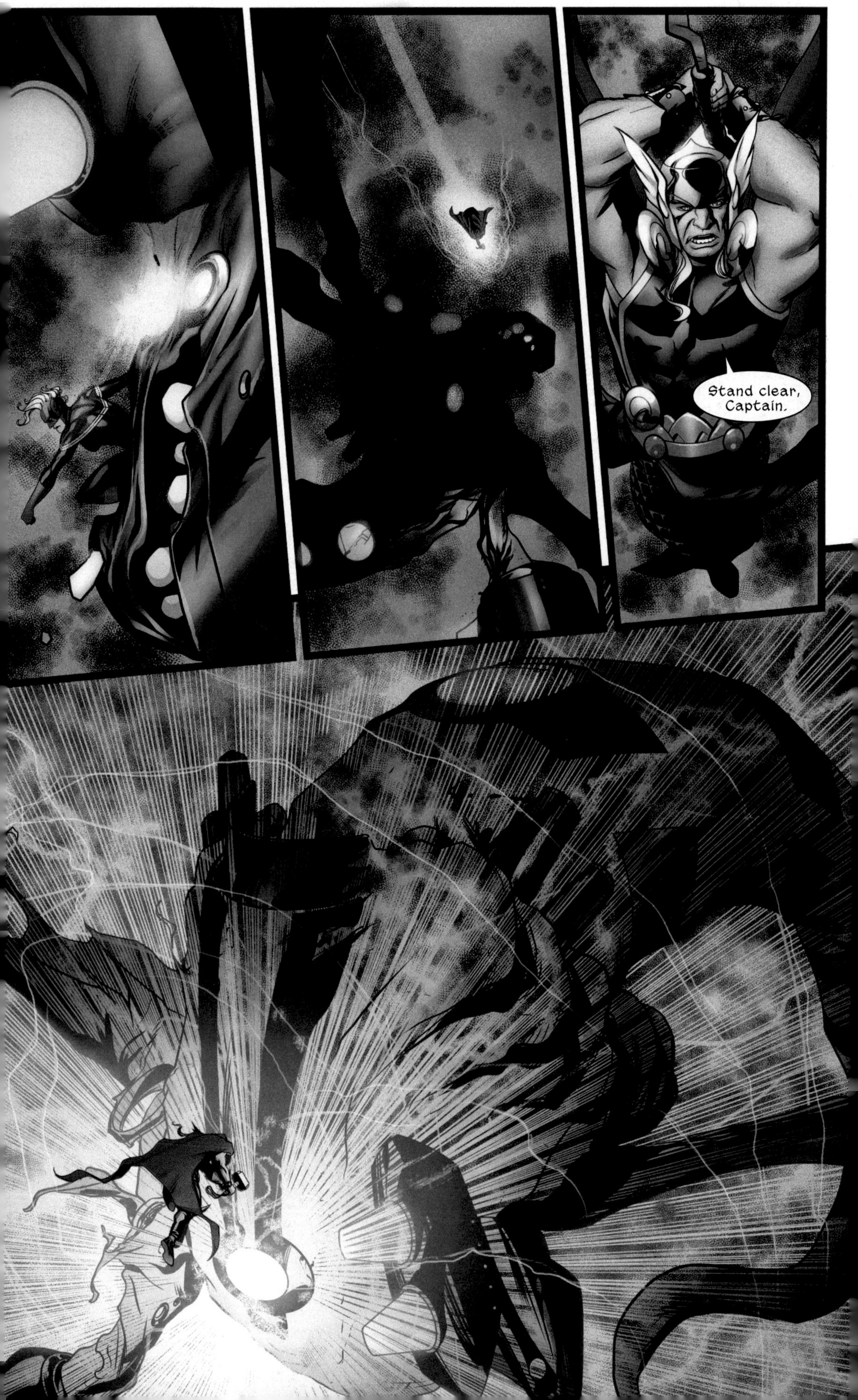
Stand clear, Captain.

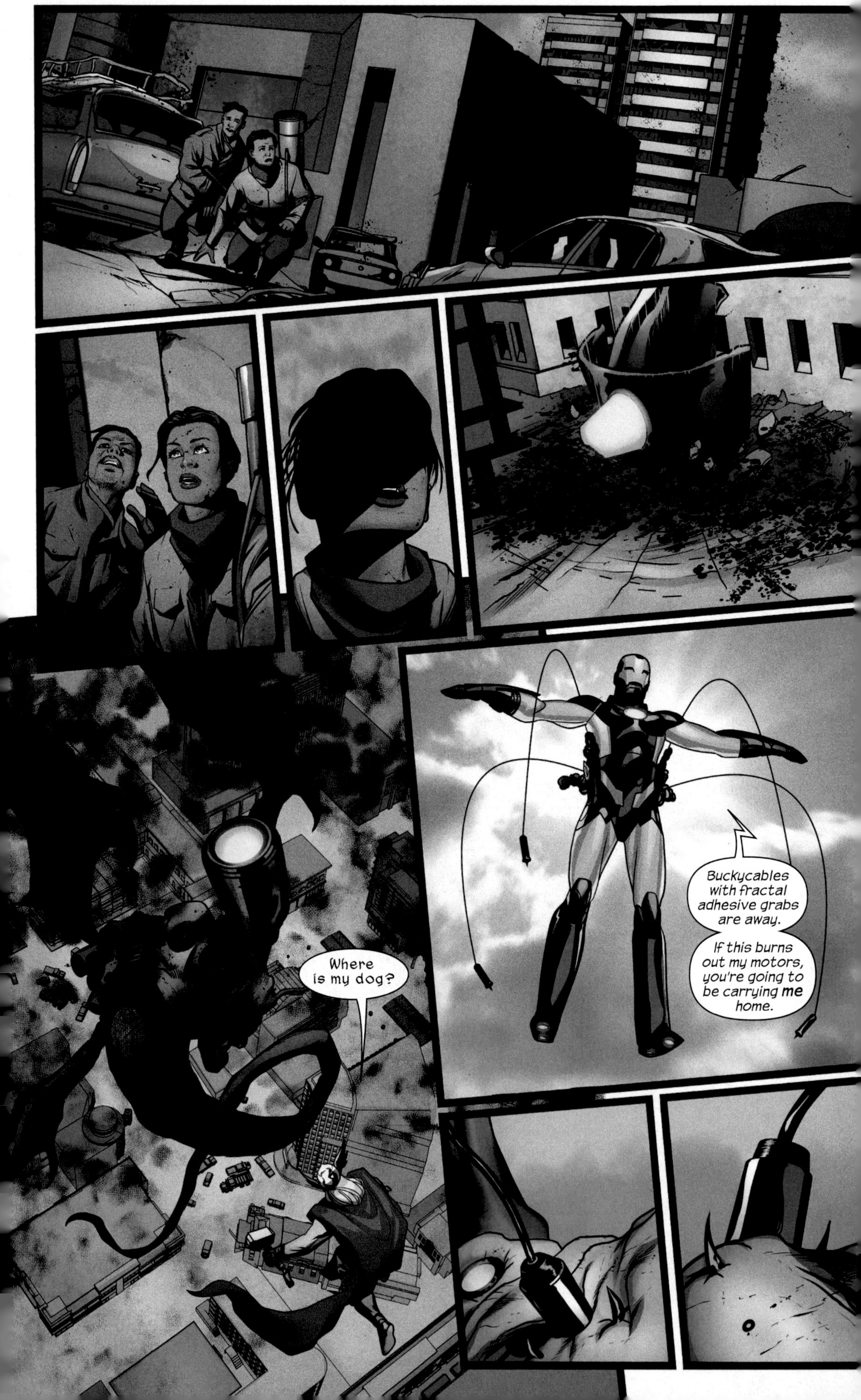
Where is my dog?
Buckycables with fractal adhesive grabs are away.
If this burns out my motors, you're going to be carrying **me** home.

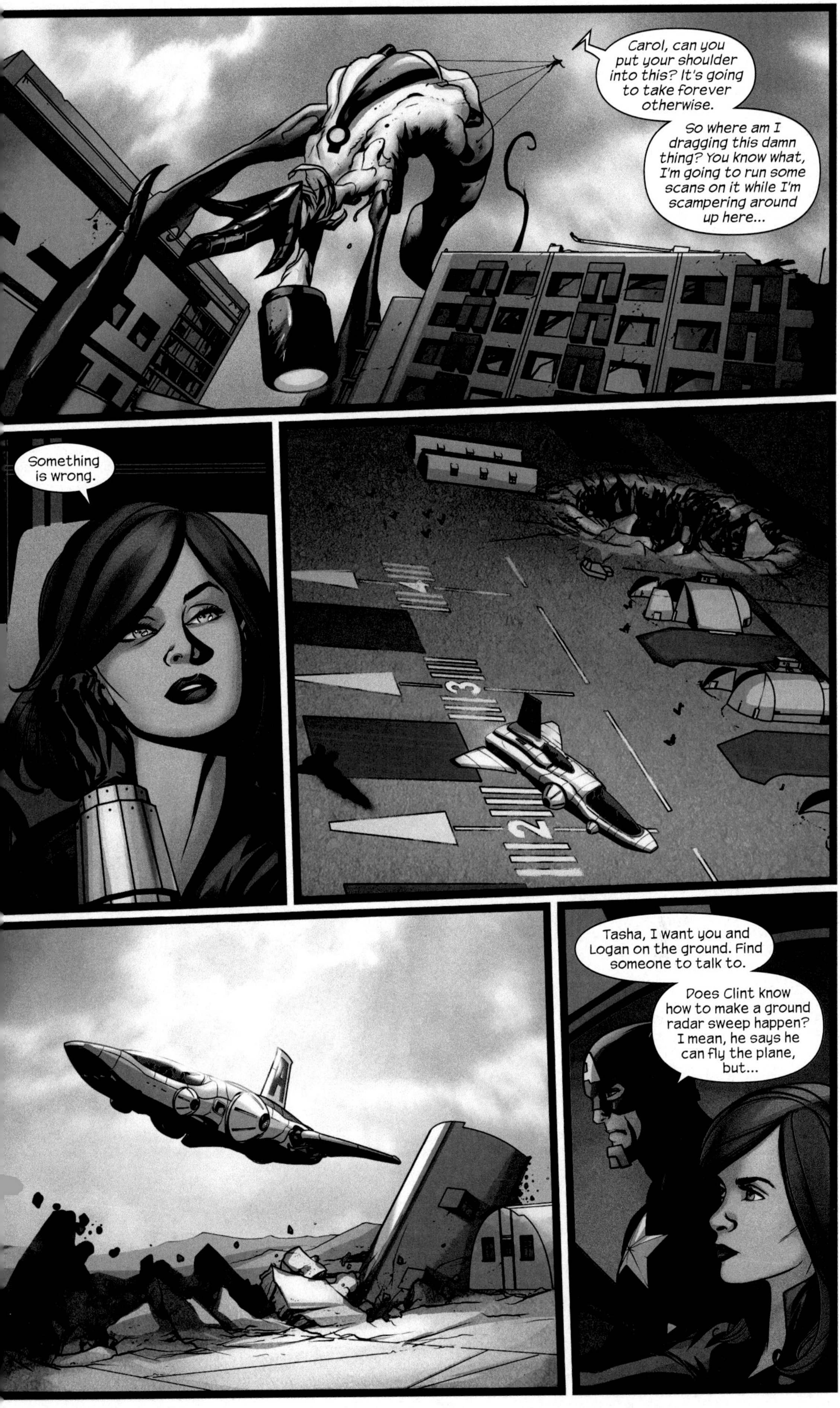
Carol, can you put your shoulder into this? It's going to take forever otherwise.
So where am I dragging this damn thing? You know what, I'm going to run some scans on it while I'm scampering around up here...
Something is wrong.
Tasha, I want you and Logan on the ground. Find someone to talk to.
Does Clint know how to make a ground radar sweep happen? I mean, he says he can fly the plane, but...

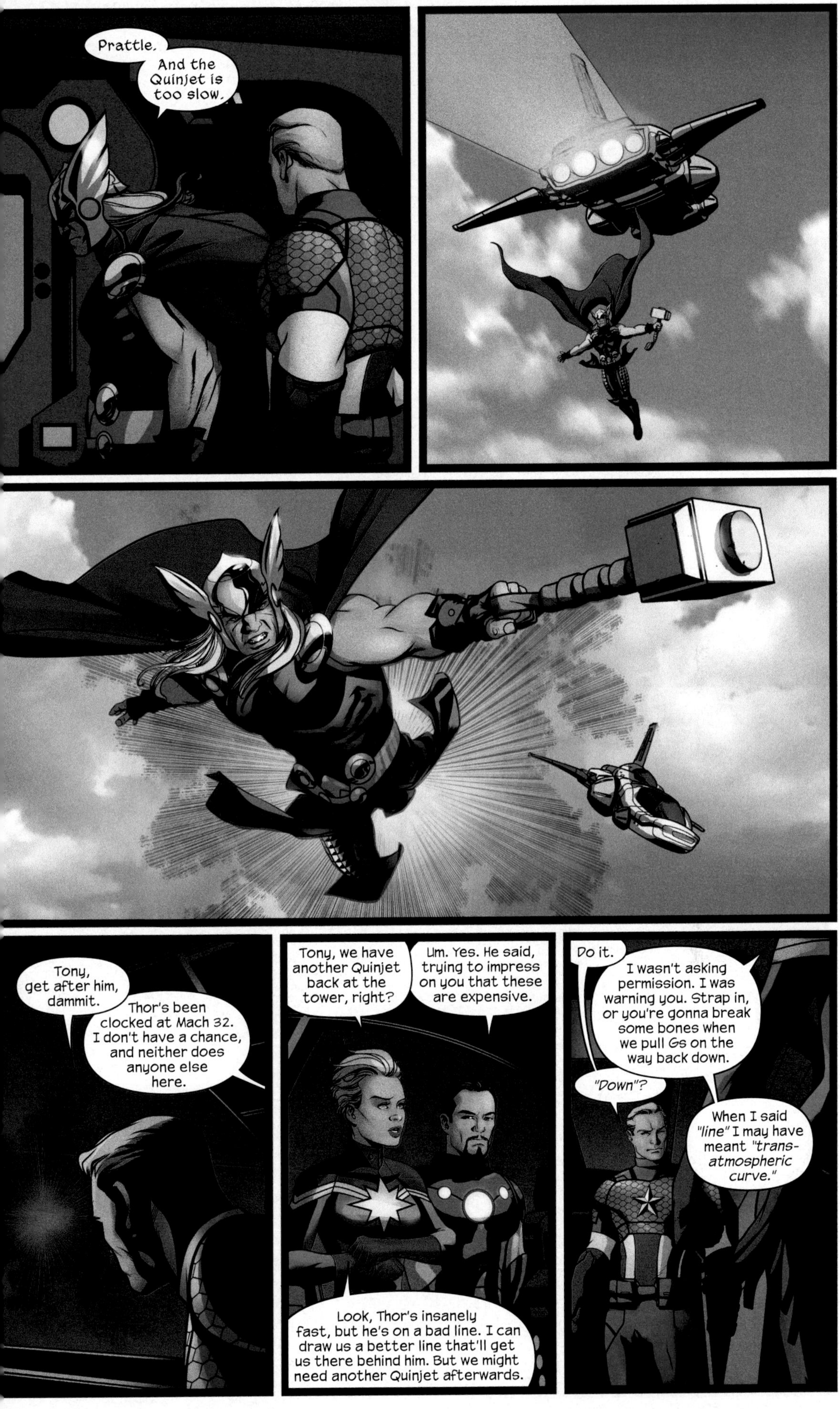
Prattle.
And the Quinjet is too slow.
Tony, get after him, dammit.
Thor's been clocked at Mach 32. I don't have a chance, and neither does anyone else here.
Tony, we have another Quinjet back at the tower, right?
Um. Yes. He said, trying to impress on you that these are expensive.
Look, Thor's insanely fast, but he's on a bad line. I can draw us a better line that'll get us there behind him. But we might need another Quinjet afterwards.
Do it.
I wasn't asking permission. I was warning you. Strap in, or you're gonna break some bones when we pull Gs on the way back down.
"Down"?
When I said *"line"* I may have meant *"trans-atmospheric curve."*

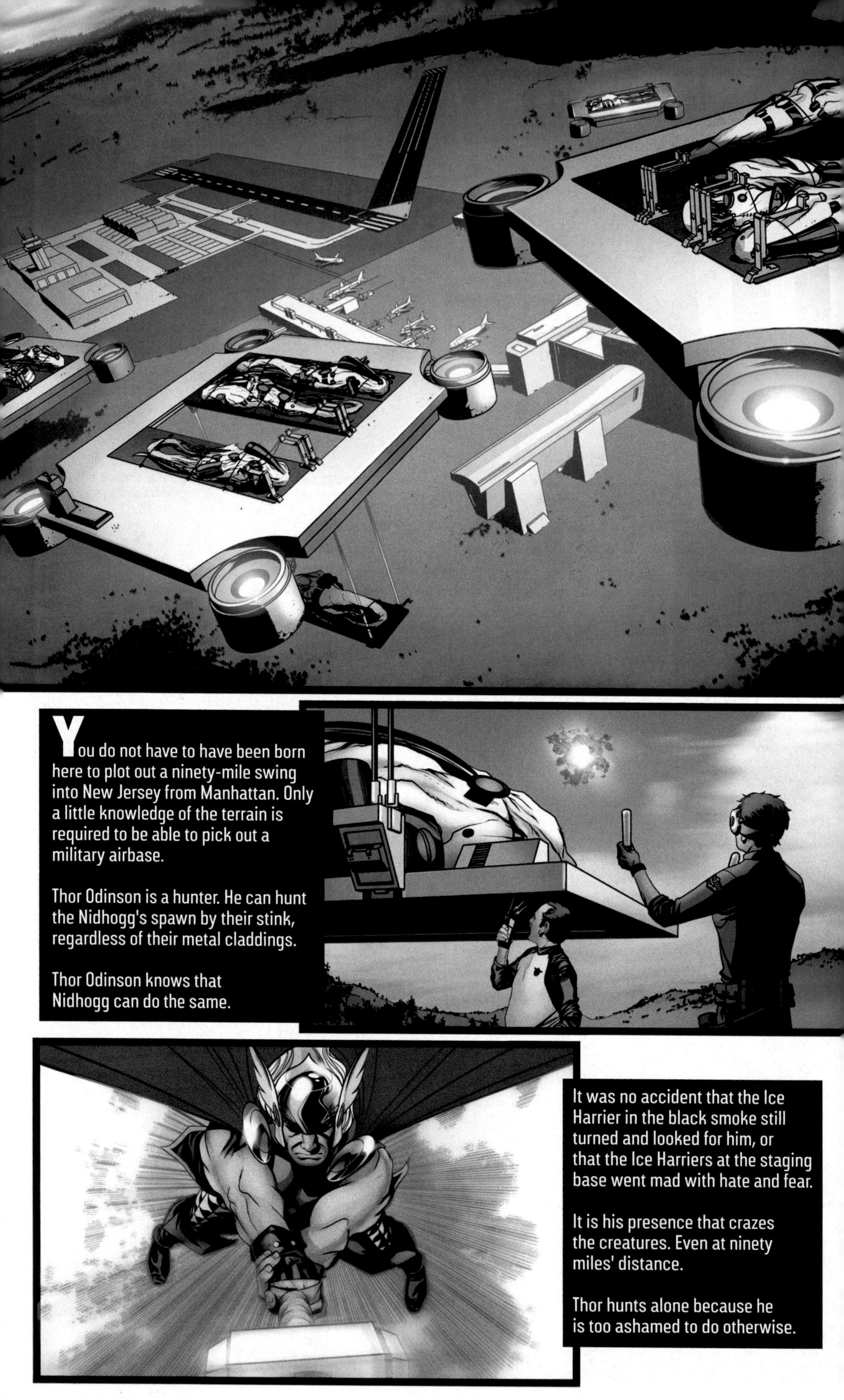
You do not have to have been born here to plot out a ninety-mile swing into New Jersey from Manhattan. Only a little knowledge of the terrain is required to be able to pick out a military airbase.
Thor Odinson is a hunter. He can hunt the Nidhogg's spawn by their stink, regardless of their metal claddings.
Thor Odinson knows that Nidhogg can do the same.
It was no accident that the Ice Harrier in the black smoke still turned and looked for him, or that the Ice Harriers at the staging base went mad with hate and fear.
It is his presence that crazes the creatures. Even at ninety miles' distance.
Thor hunts alone because he is too ashamed to do otherwise.

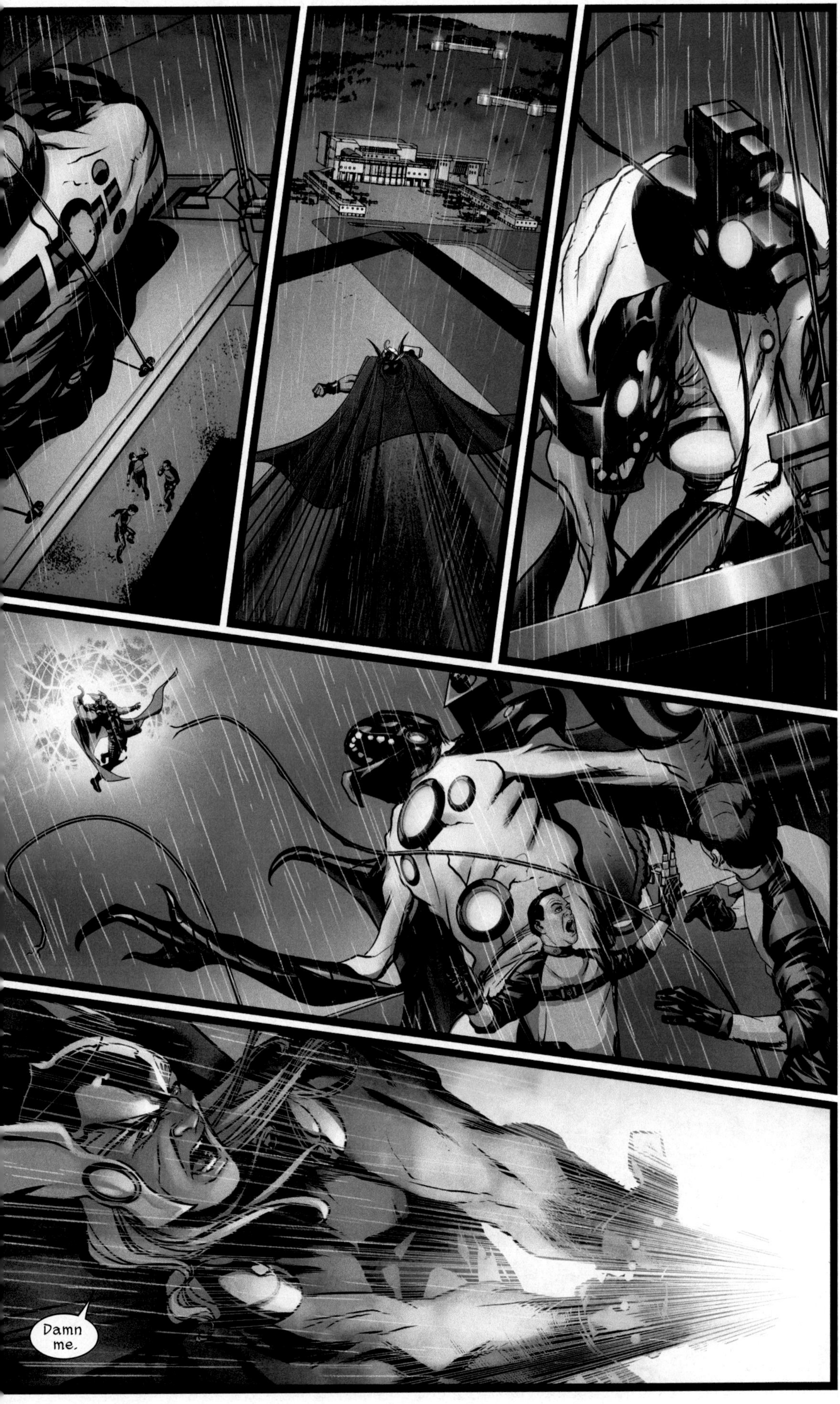
Damn me.

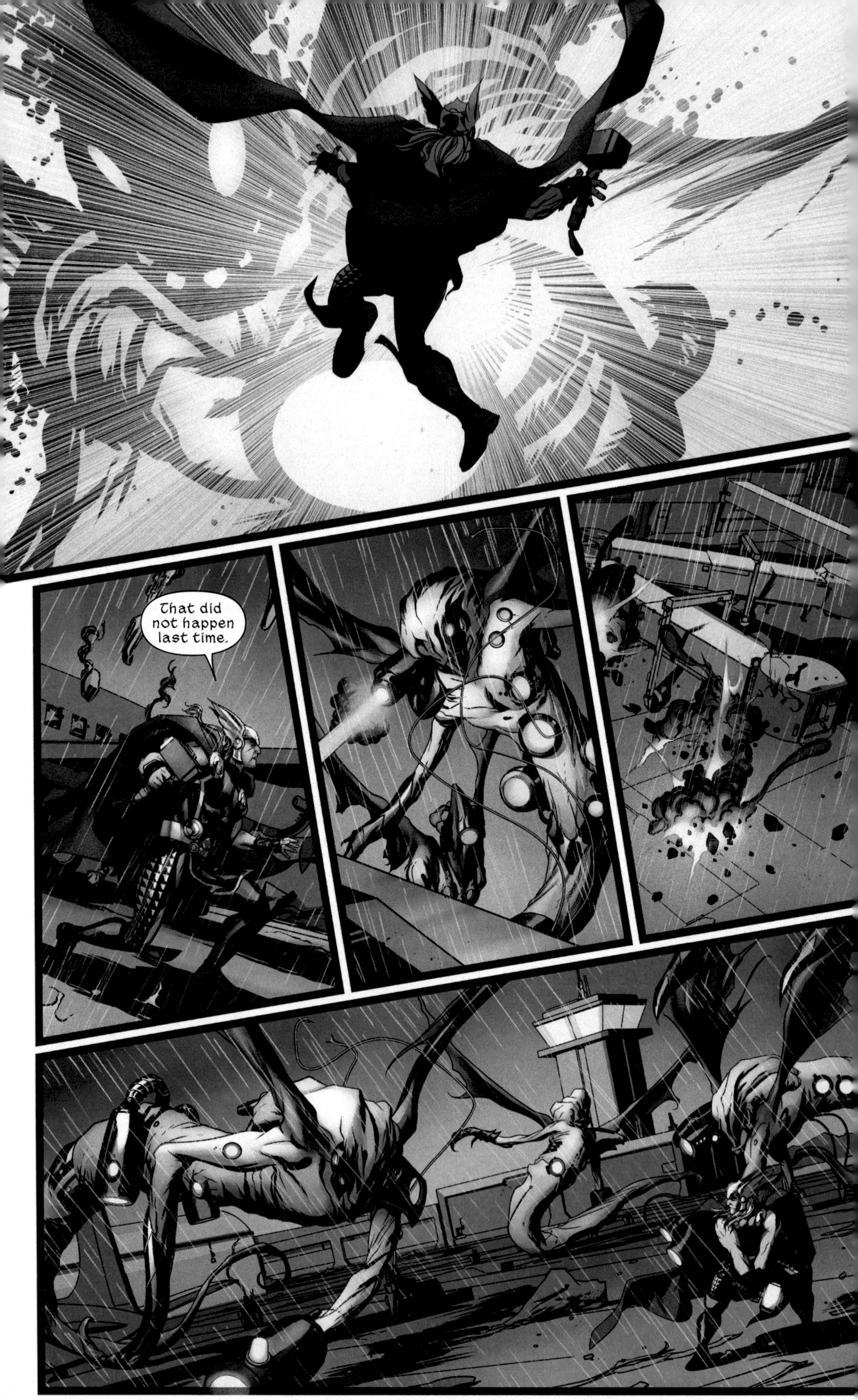
That did not happen last time.

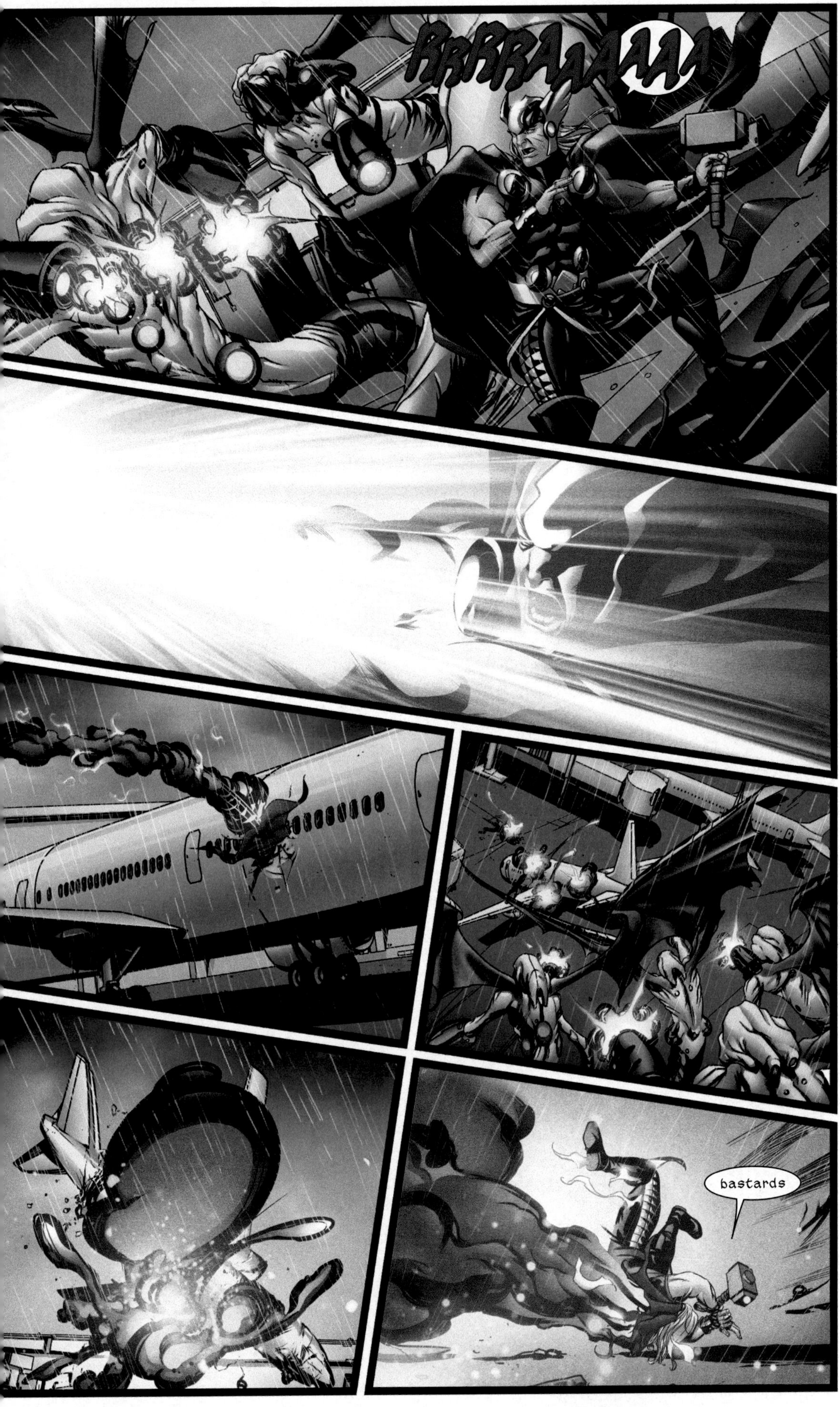
RRRRAAAAAA
bastards

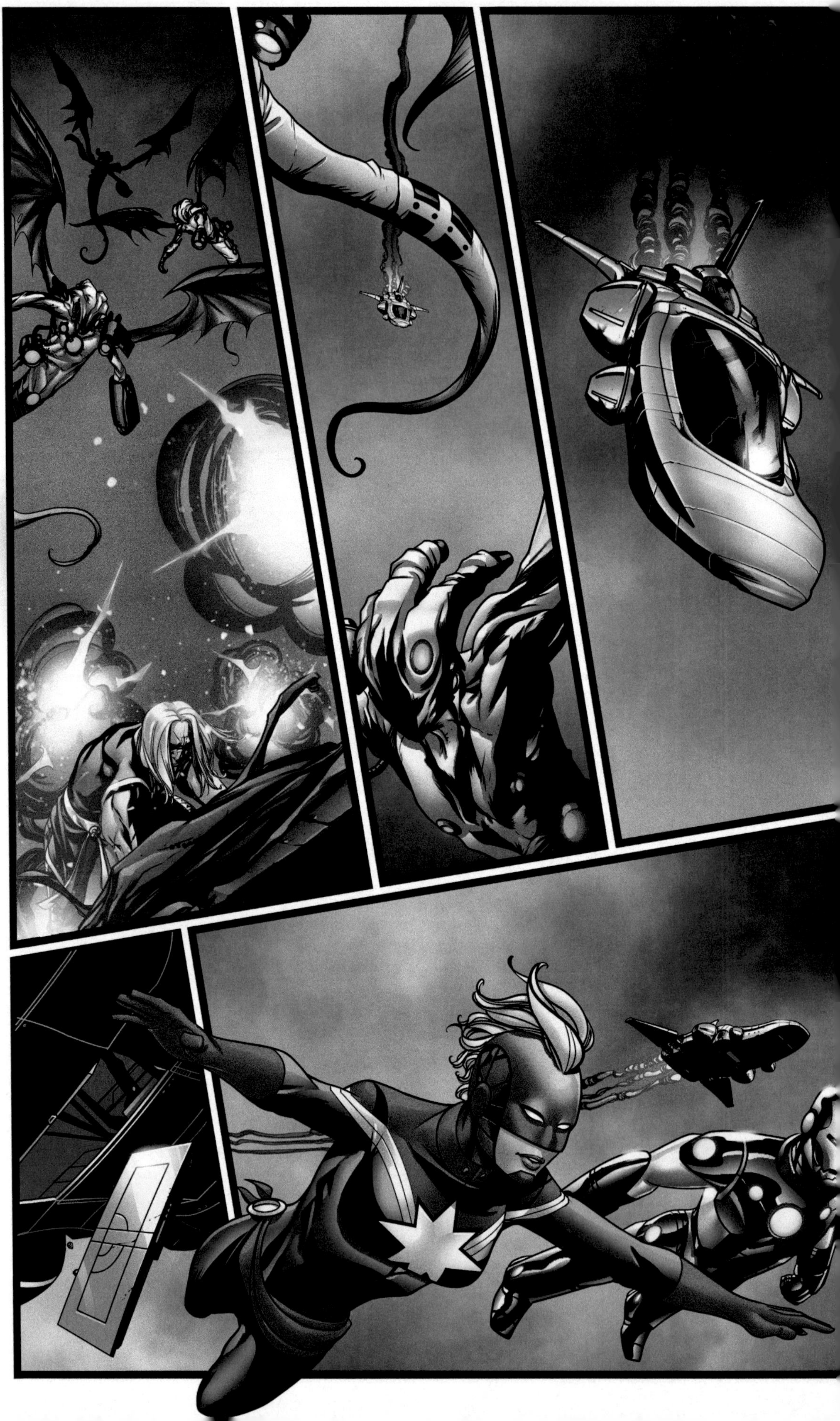

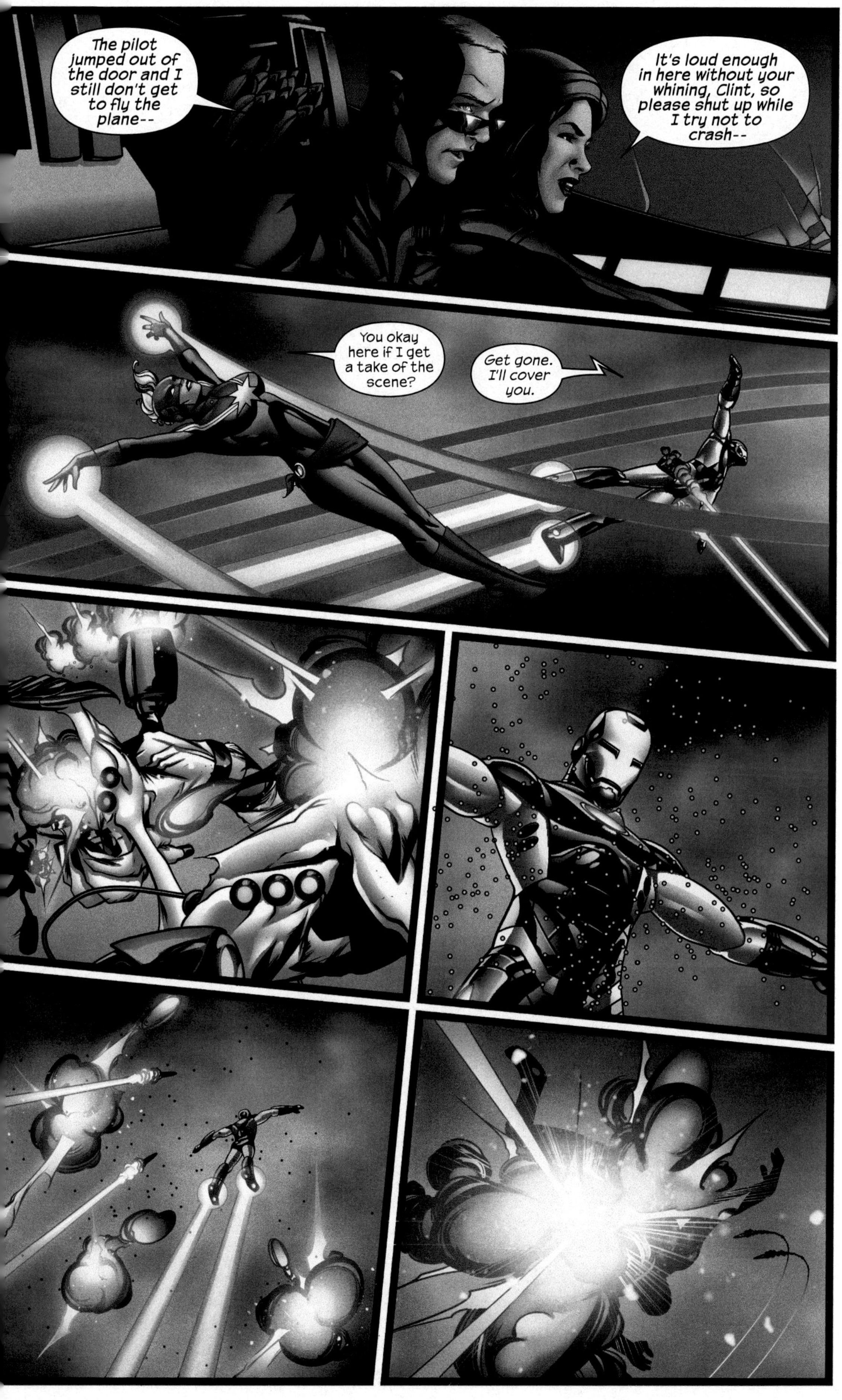

The pilot jumped out of the door and I still don't get to fly the plane--
It's loud enough in here without your whining, Clint, so please shut up while I try not to crash--
You okay here if I get a take of the scene?
Get gone. I'll cover you.

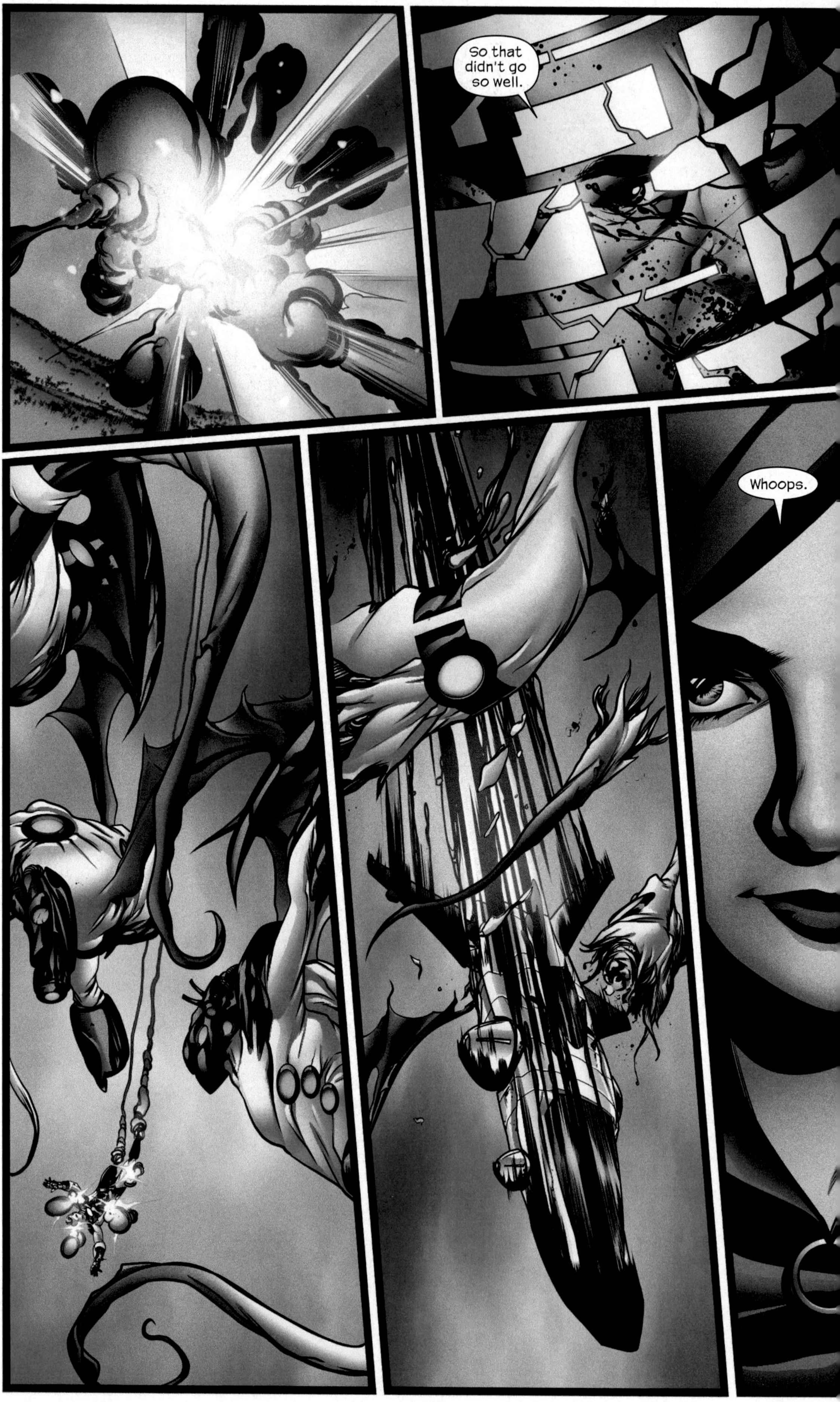
So that didn't go so well.
Whoops.

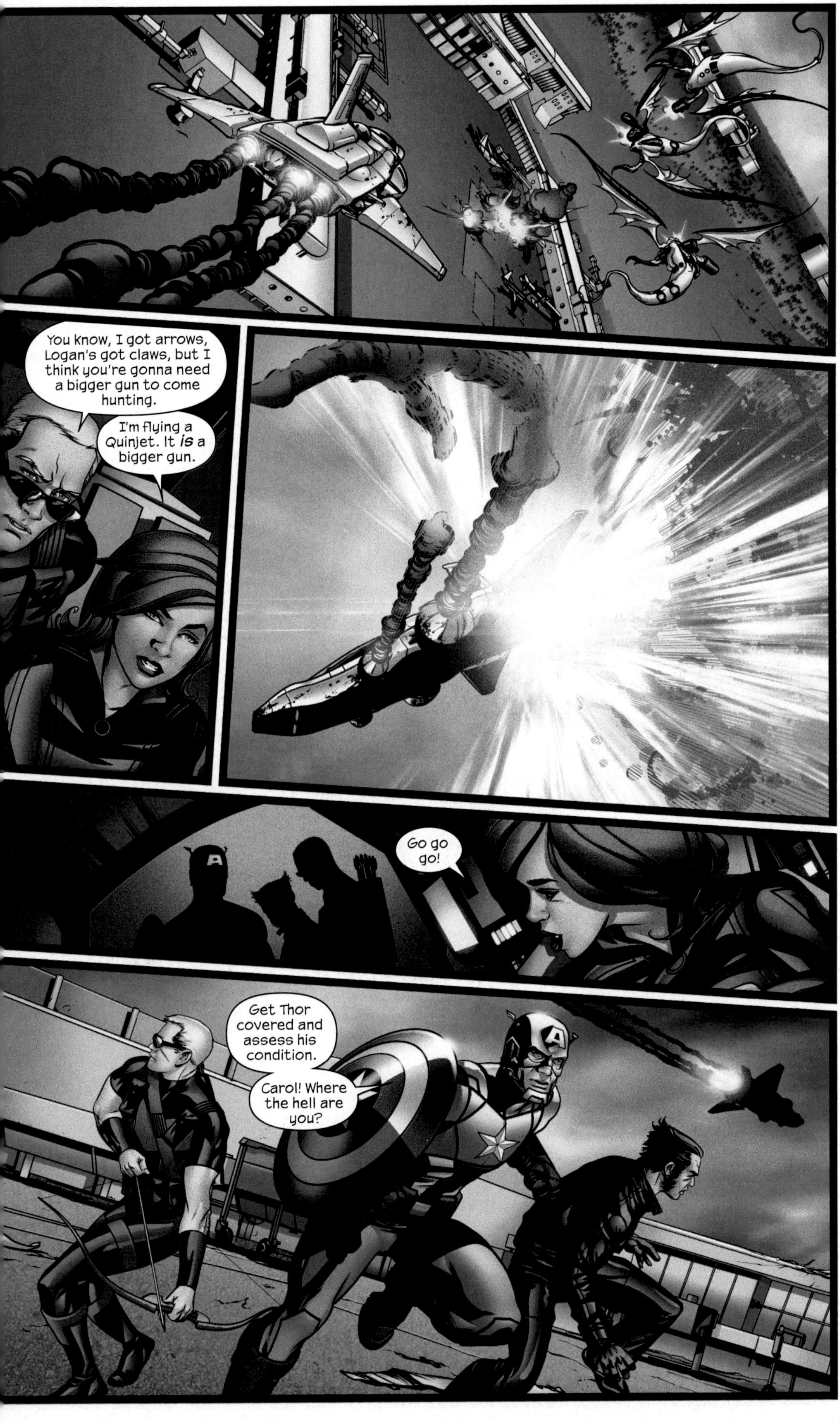
You know, I got arrows, Logan's got claws, but I think you're gonna need a bigger gun to come hunting.
I'm flying a Quinjet. It *is* a bigger gun.
Go go go!
Get Thor covered and assess his condition.
Carol! Where the hell are you?

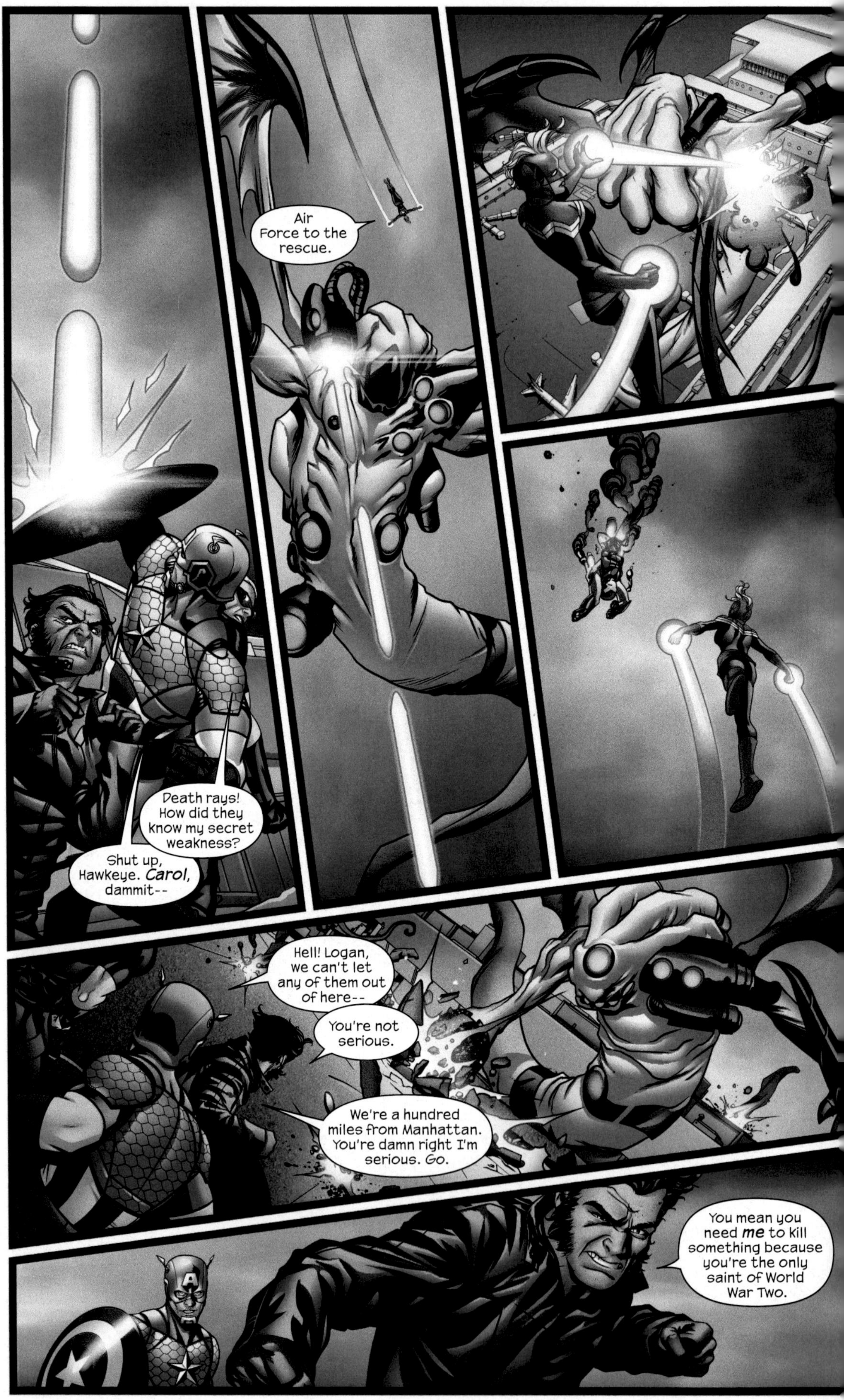
Air Force to the rescue.
Death rays! How did they know my secret weakness?
Shut up, Hawkeye. Carol, dammit--
Hell! Logan, we can't let any of them out of here--
You're not serious.
We're a hundred miles from Manhattan. You're damn right I'm serious. Go.
You mean you need me to kill something because you're the only saint of World War Two.

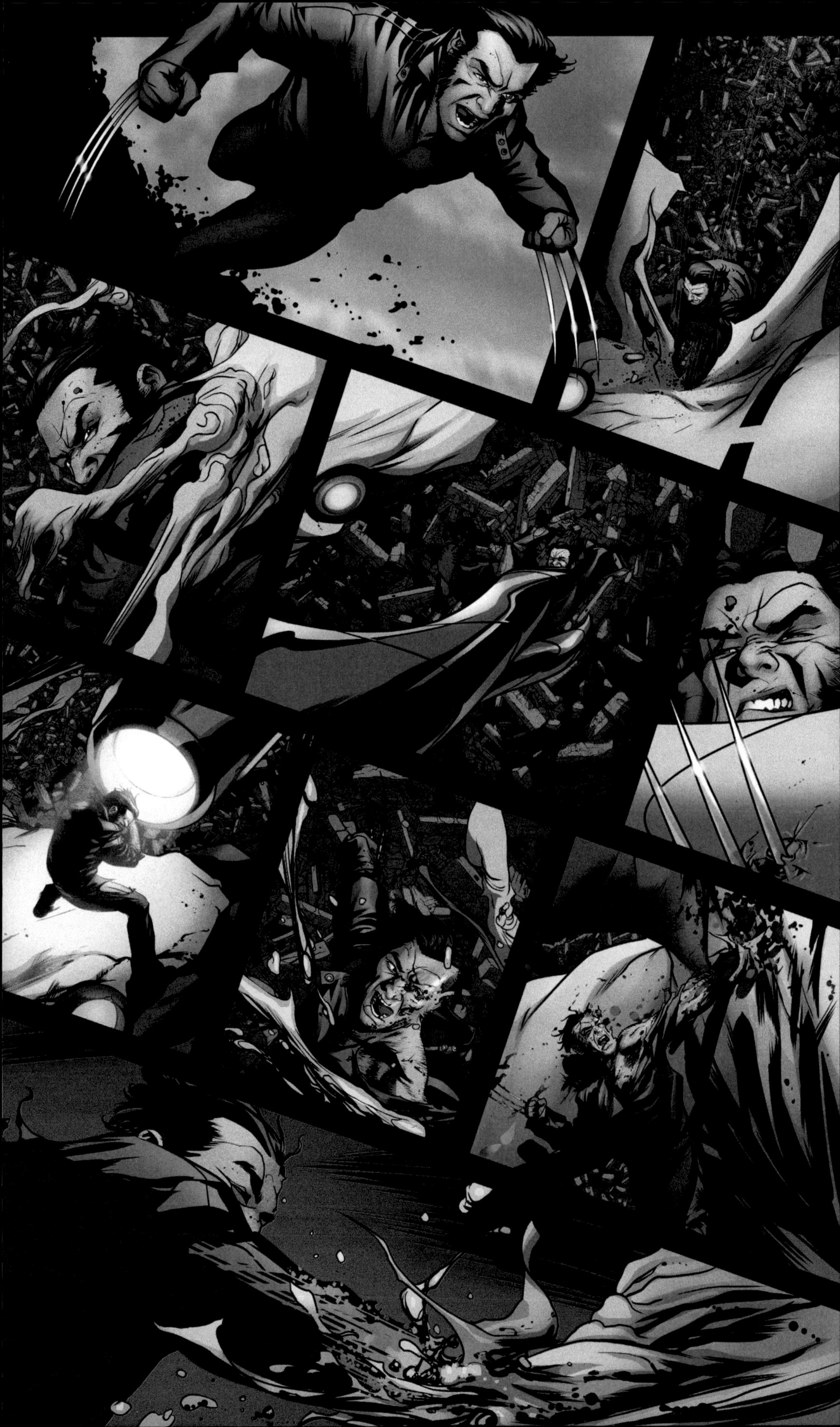

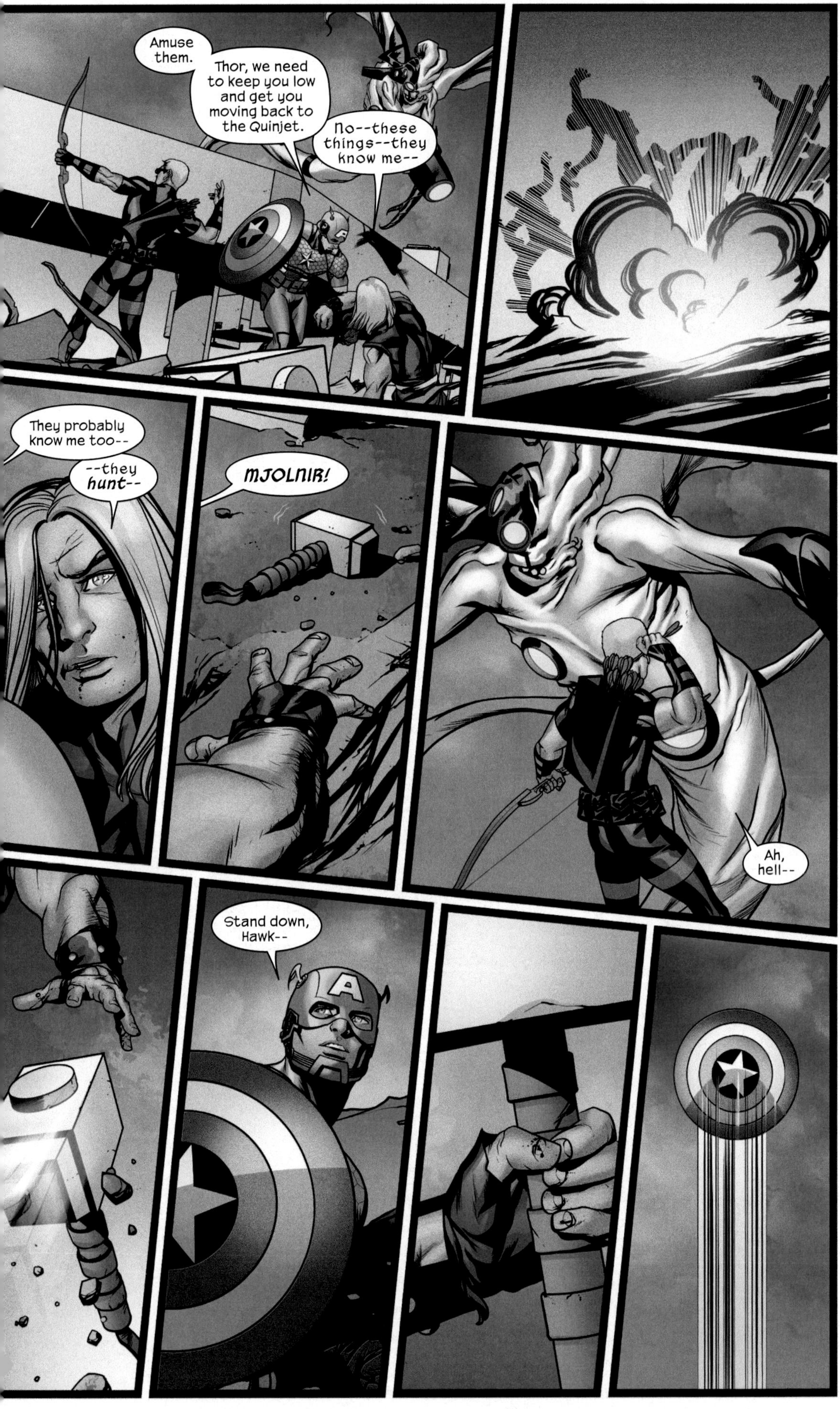
Amuse them.
Thor, we need to keep you low and get you moving back to the Quinjet.
No--these things--they know me--
They probably know me too--
--they *hunt*--
MJOLNIR!
Ah, hell--
Stand down, Hawk--

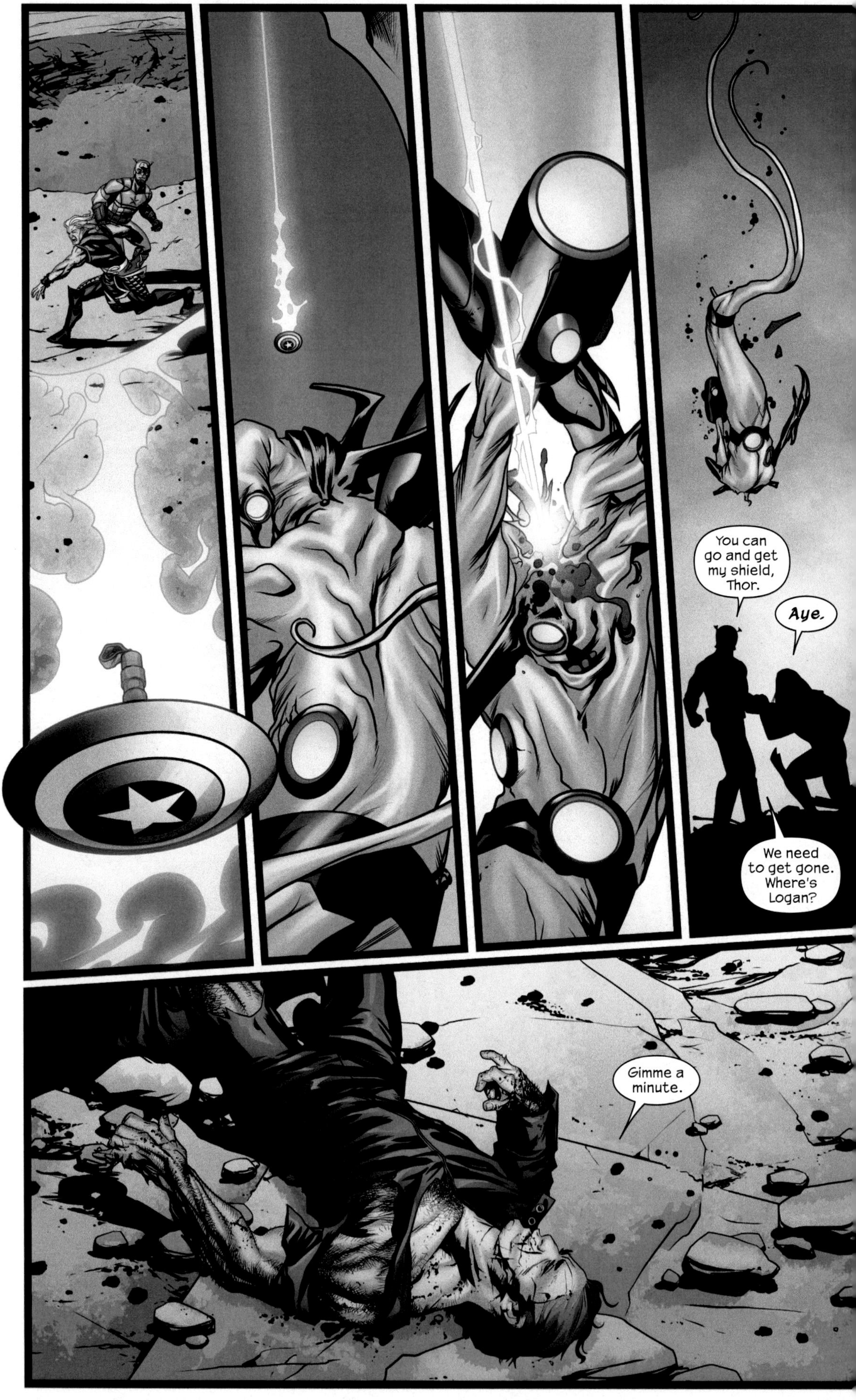
You can go and get my shield, Thor.
Aye.
We need to get gone. Where's Logan?
Gimme a minute.

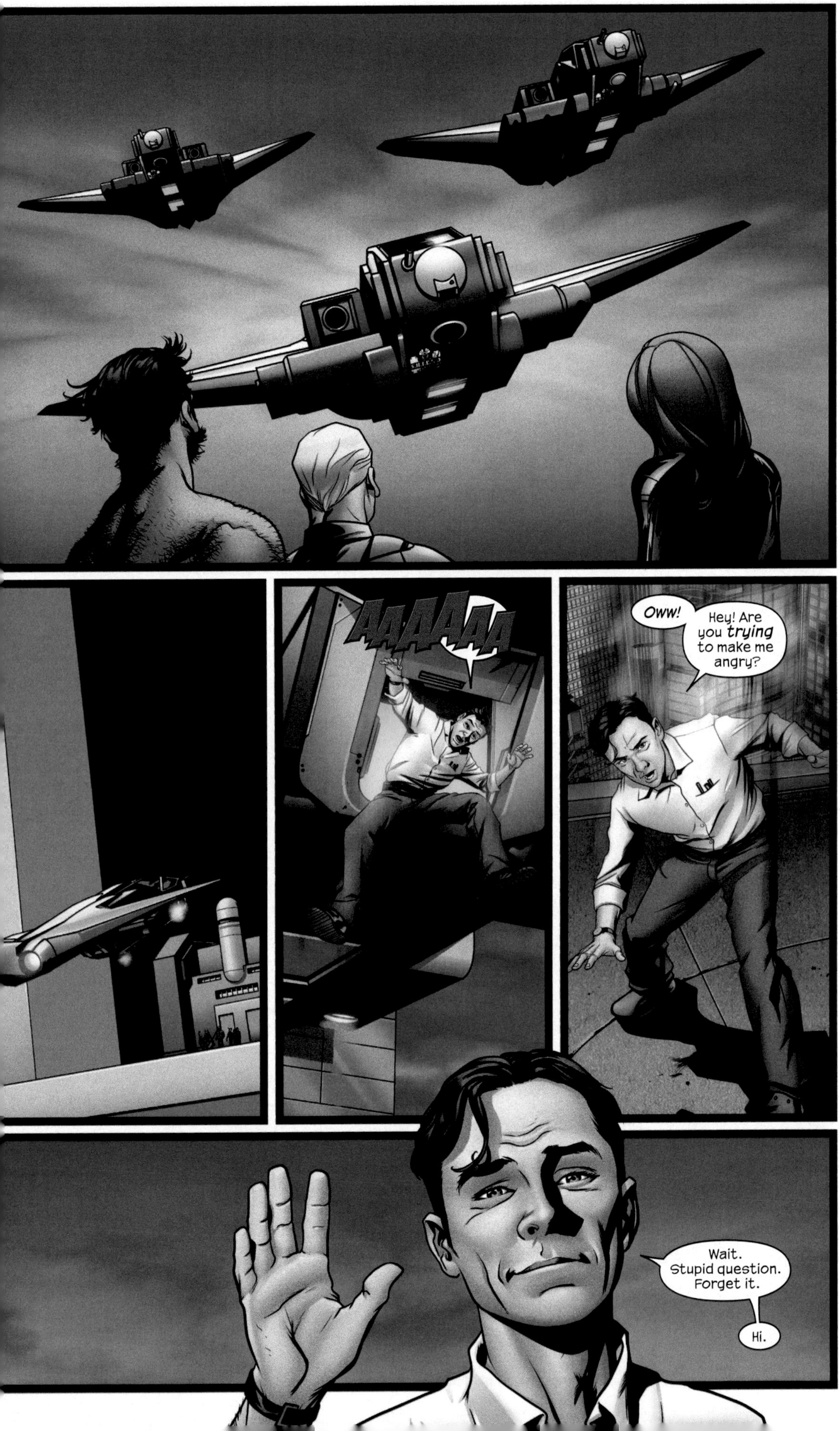
AAAAAA
Oww!
Hey! Are you *trying* to make me angry?
Wait. Stupid question. Forget it.
Hi.

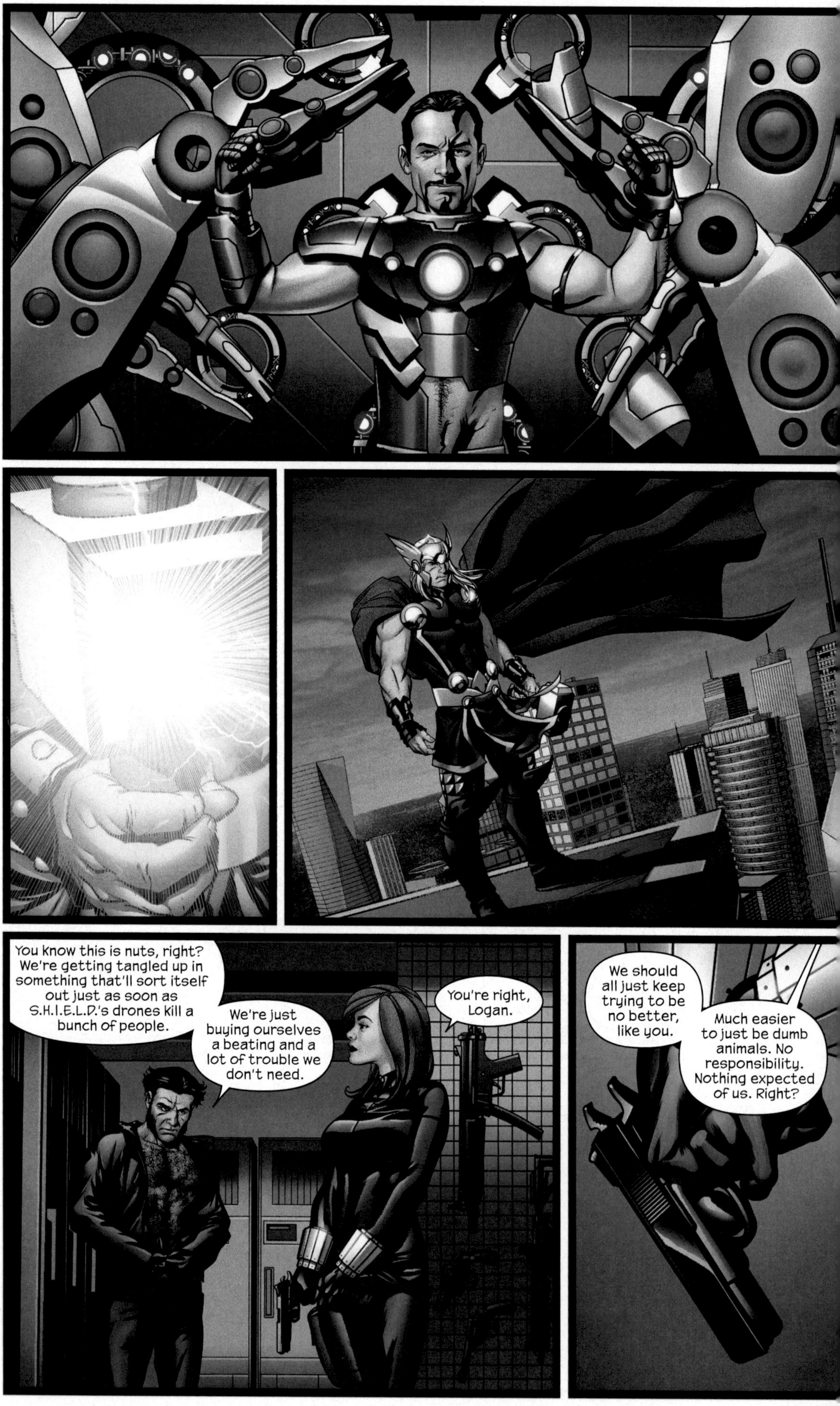
You know this is nuts, right? We're getting tangled up in something that'll sort itself out just as soon as S.H.I.E.L.D.'s drones kill a bunch of people.
We're just buying ourselves a beating and a lot of trouble we don't need.
You're right, Logan.
We should all just keep trying to be no better, like you.
Much easier to just be dumb animals. No responsibility. Nothing expected of us. Right?

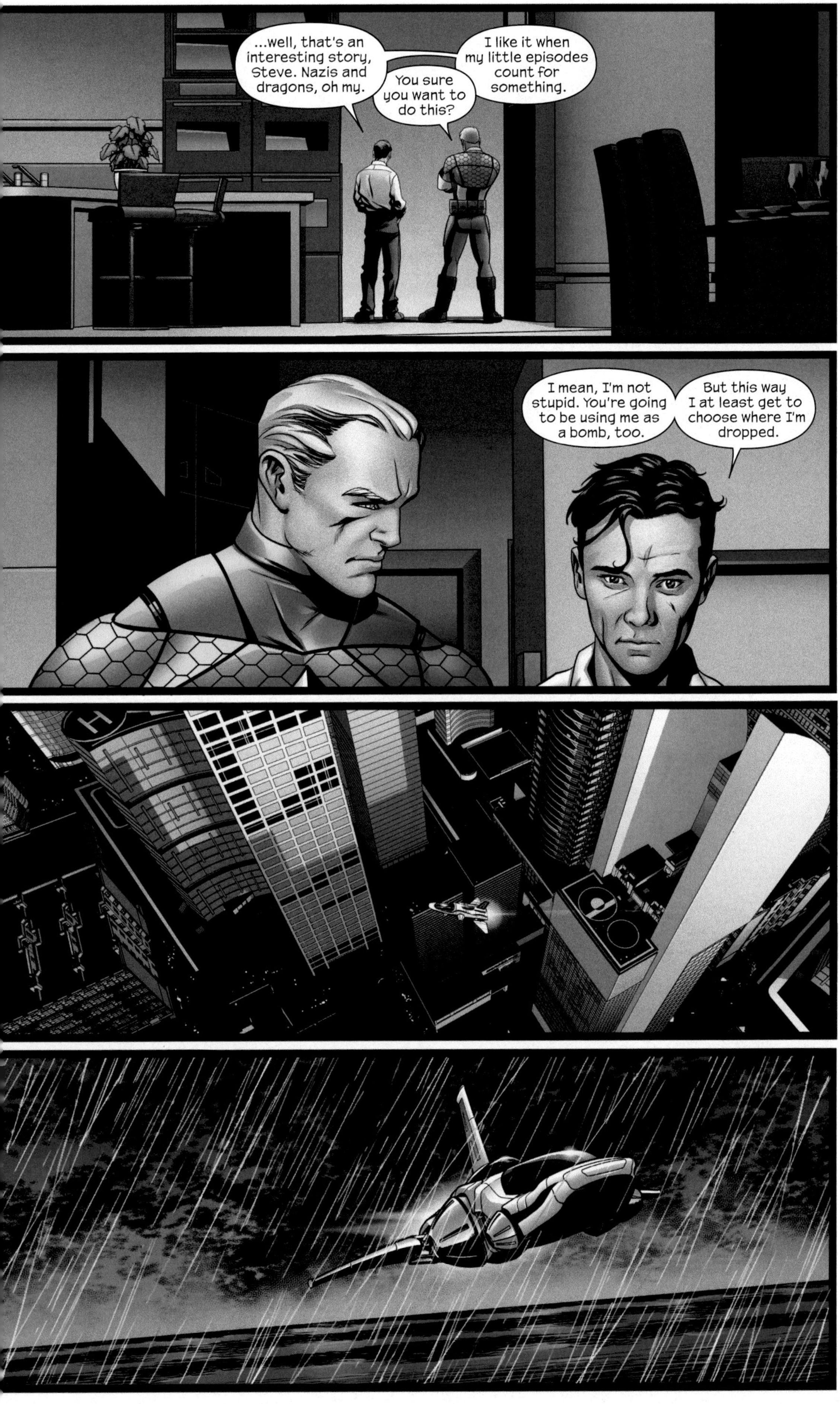
...well, that's an interesting story, Steve. Nazis and dragons, oh my.
You sure you want to do this?
I like it when my little episodes count for something.
I mean, I'm not stupid. You're going to be using me as a bomb, too.
But this way I at least get to choose where I'm dropped.

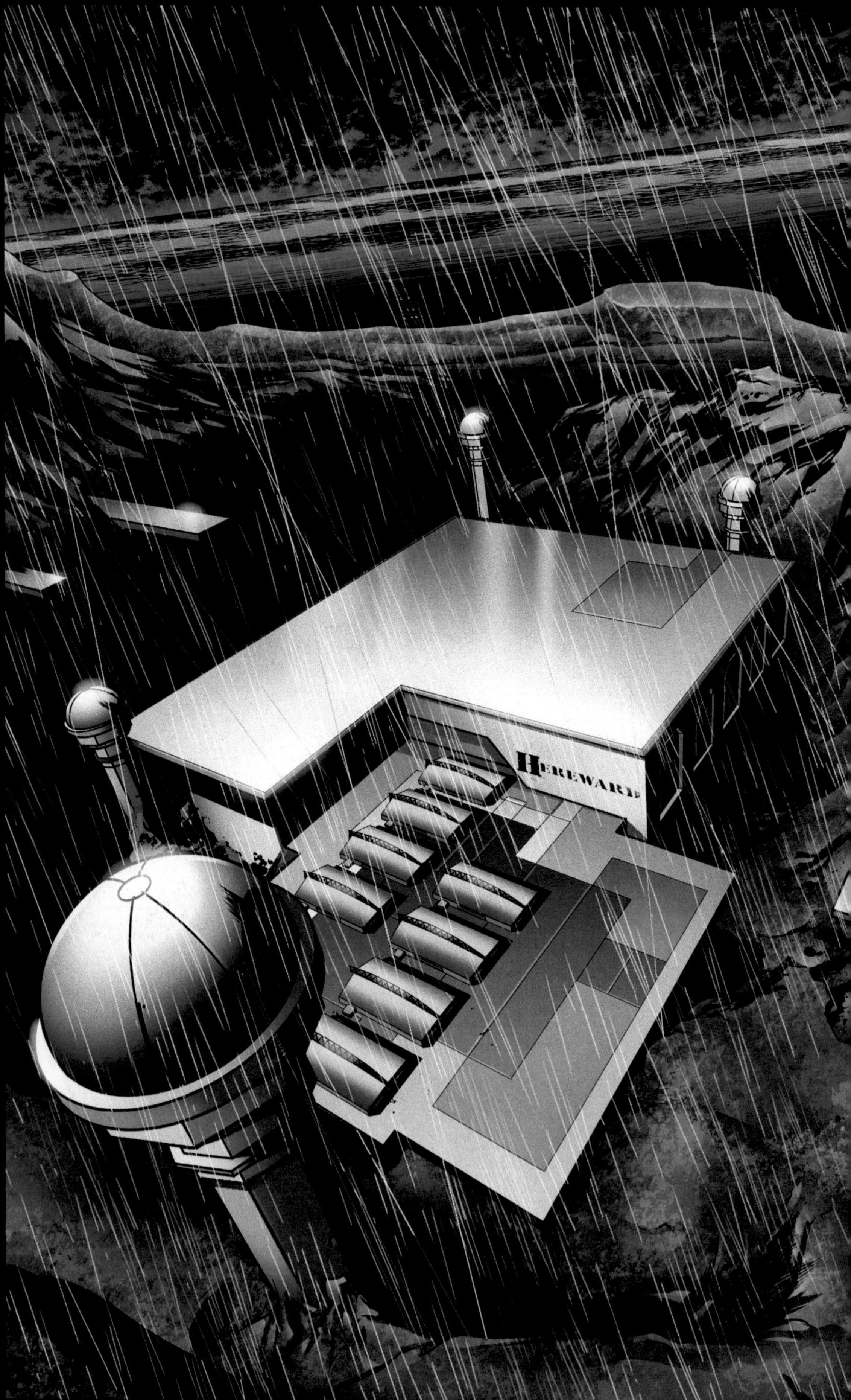
HEREWARD

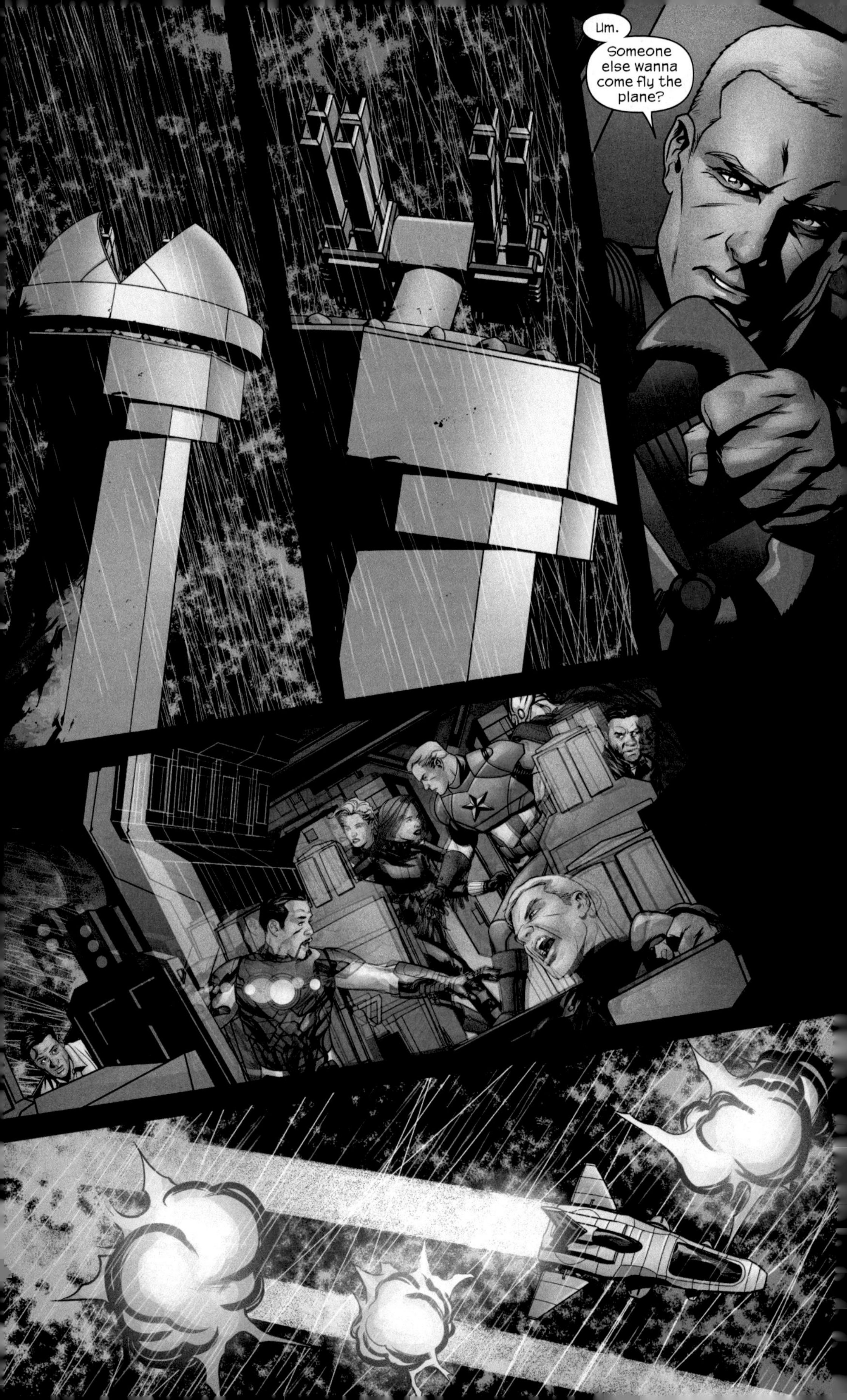
Um.
Someone else wanna come fly the plane?

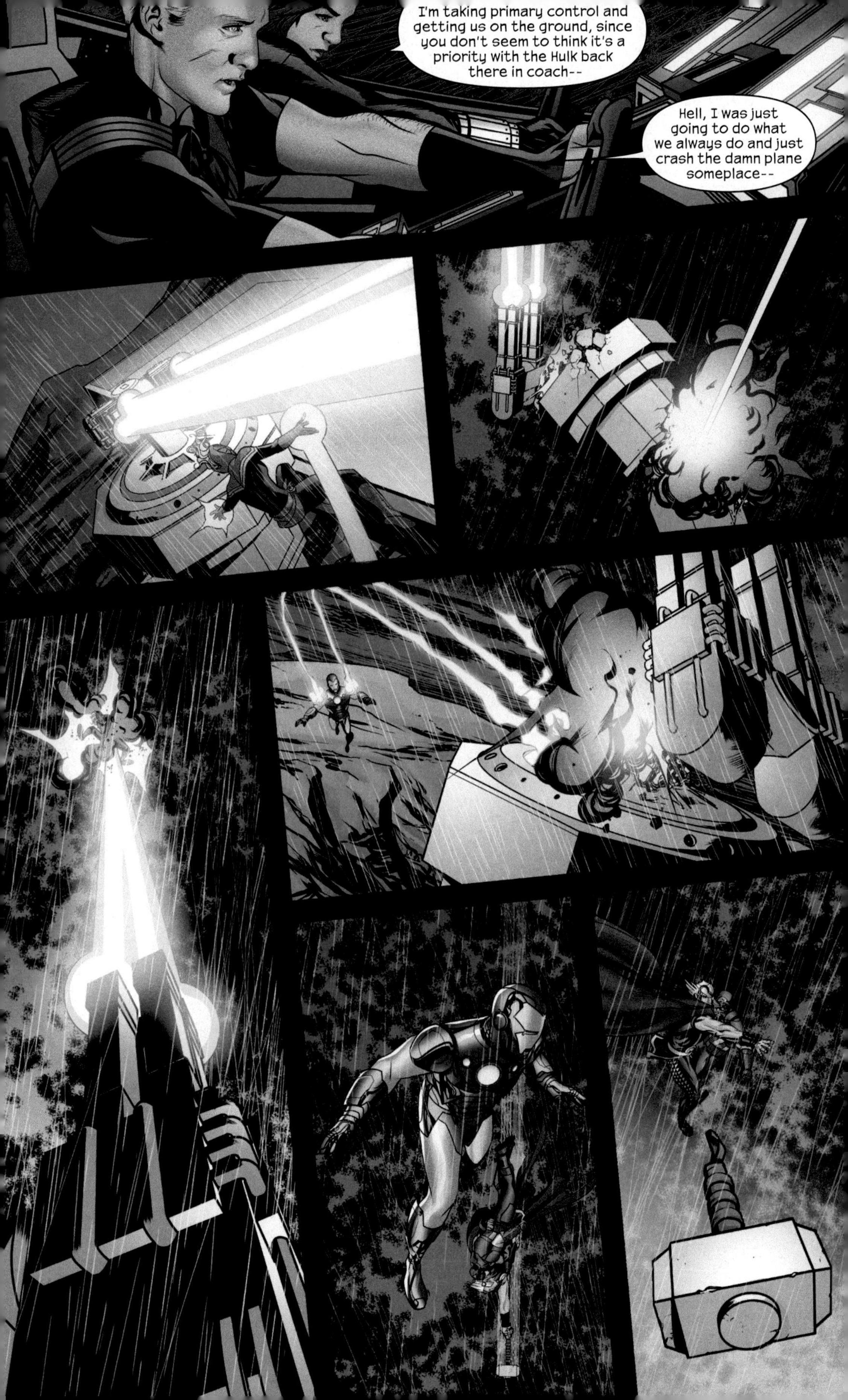
I'm taking primary control and getting us on the ground, since you don't seem to think it's a priority with the Hulk back there in coach--
Hell, I was just going to do what we always do and just crash the damn plane someplace--

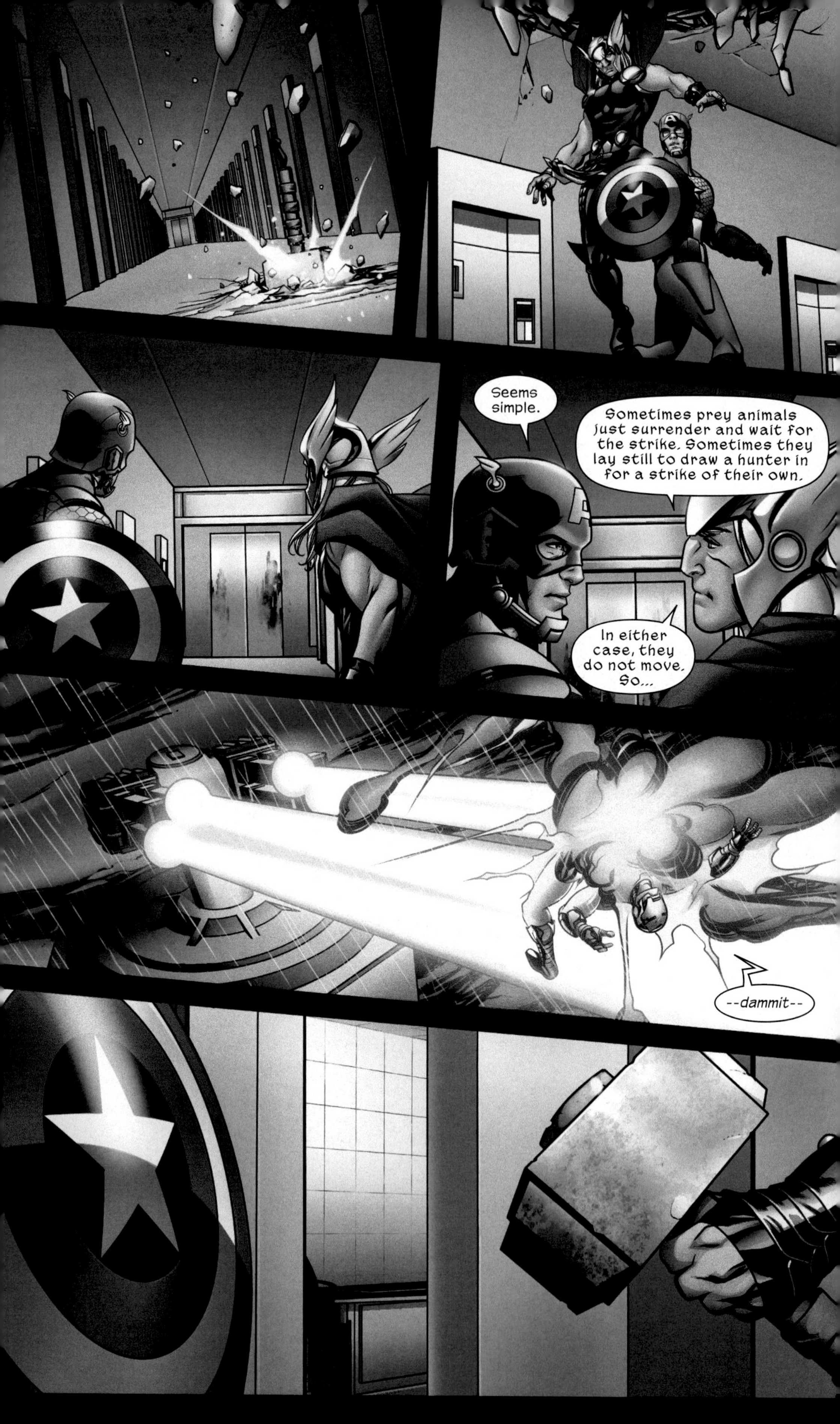
Seems simple.
Sometimes prey animals just surrender and wait for the strike. Sometimes they lay still to draw a hunter in for a strike of their own.
In either case, they do not move. So...
--dammit--

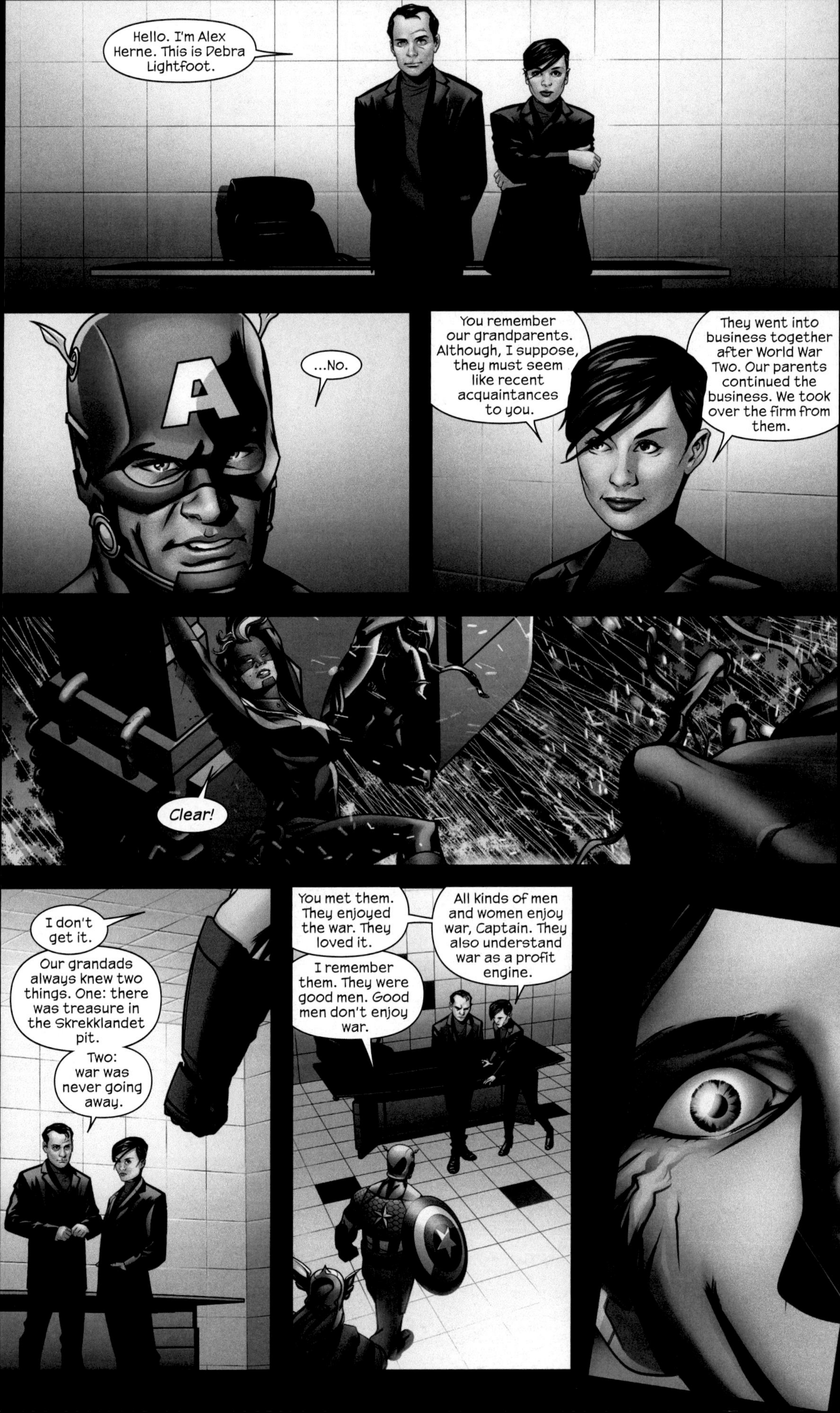
Hello. I'm Alex Herne. This is Debra Lightfoot.
...No.
You remember our grandparents. Although, I suppose, they must seem like recent acquaintances to you.
They went into business together after World War Two. Our parents continued the business. We took over the firm from them.
Clear!
I don't get it.
Our grandads always knew two things. One: there was treasure in the Skrekklandet pit.
Two: war was never going away.
You met them. They enjoyed the war. They loved it.
I remember them. They were good men. Good men don't enjoy war.
All kinds of men and women enjoy war, Captain. They also understand war as a profit engine.

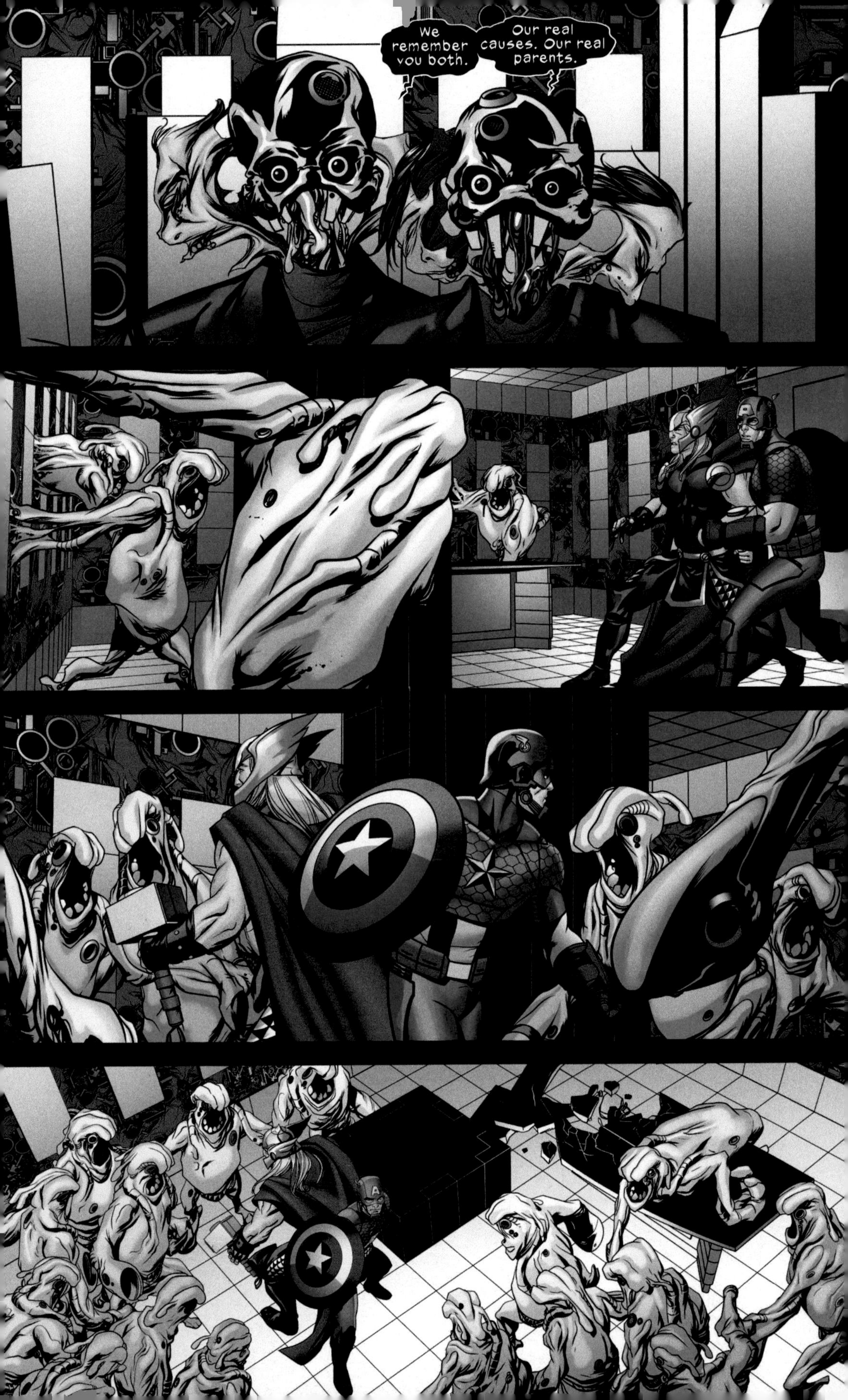
We remember you both.
Our real causes. Our real parents.

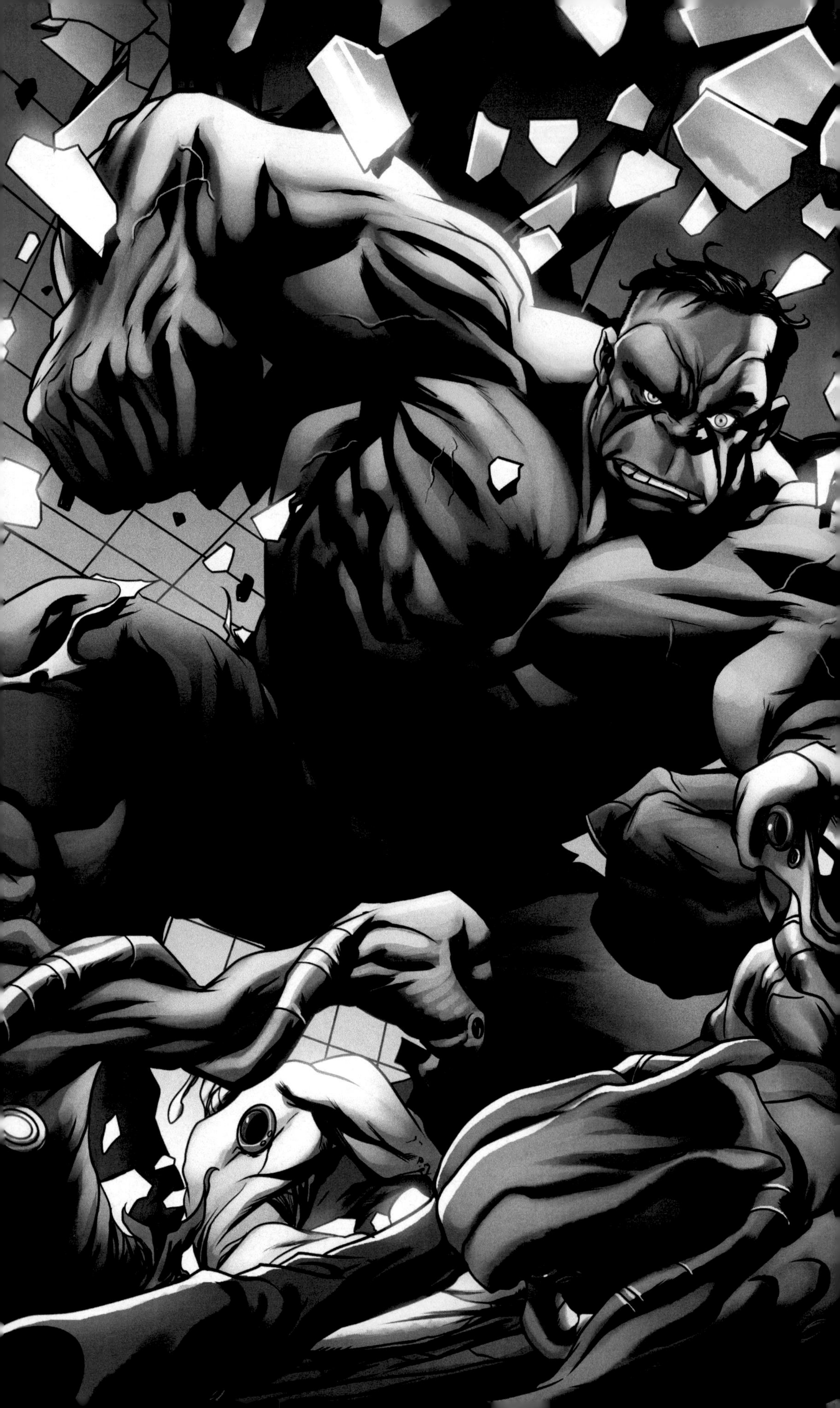

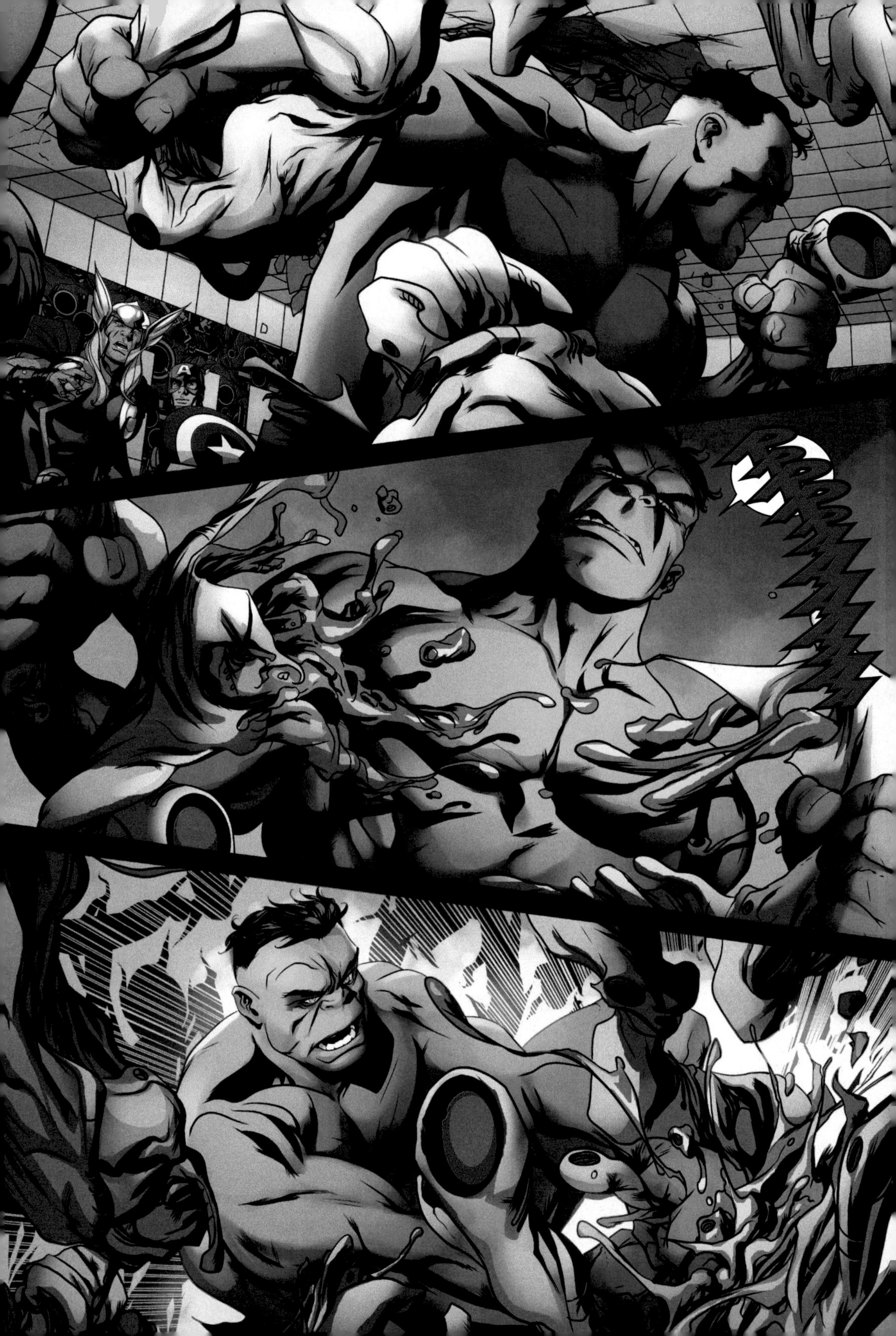

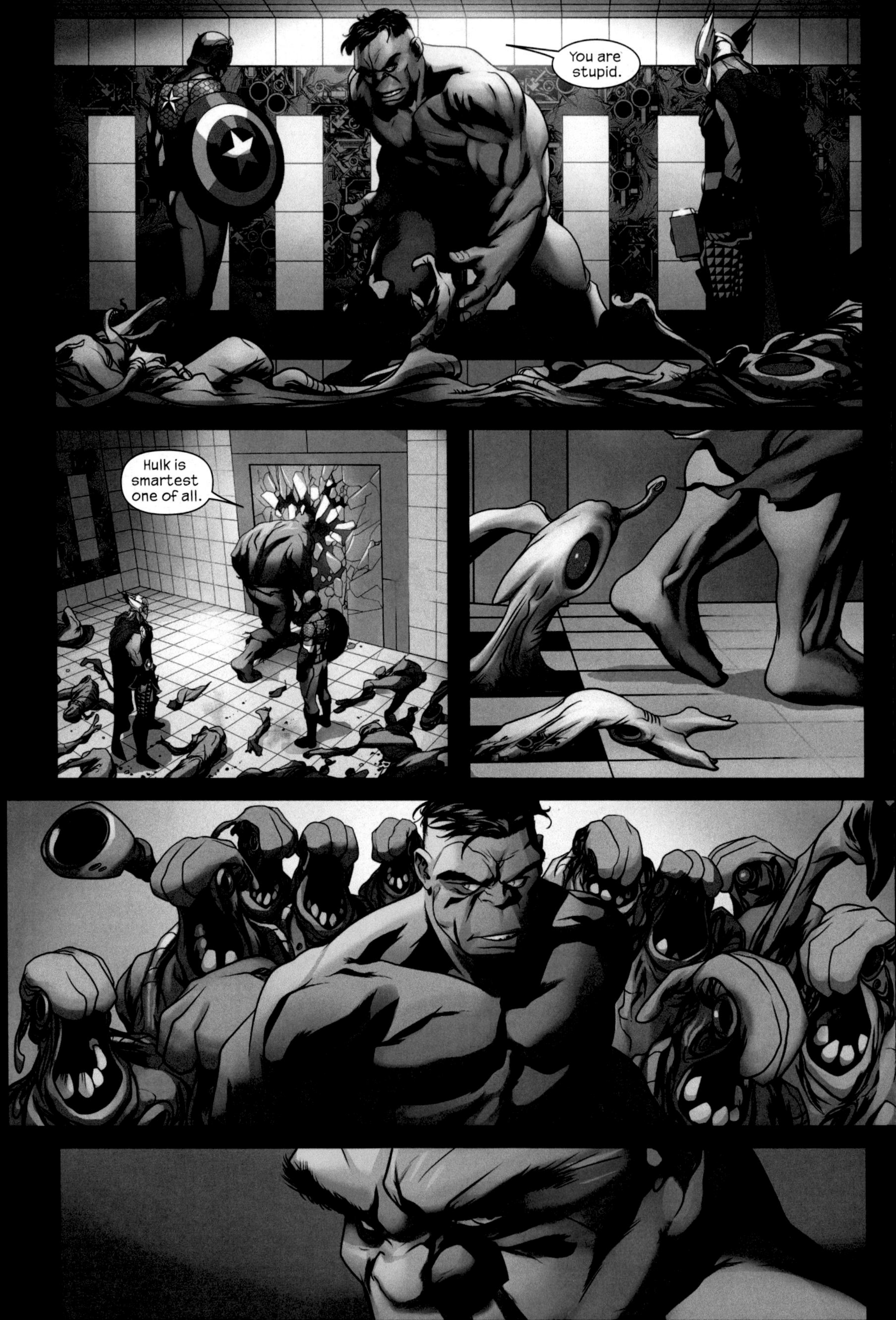
You are stupid.
Hulk is smartest one of all.

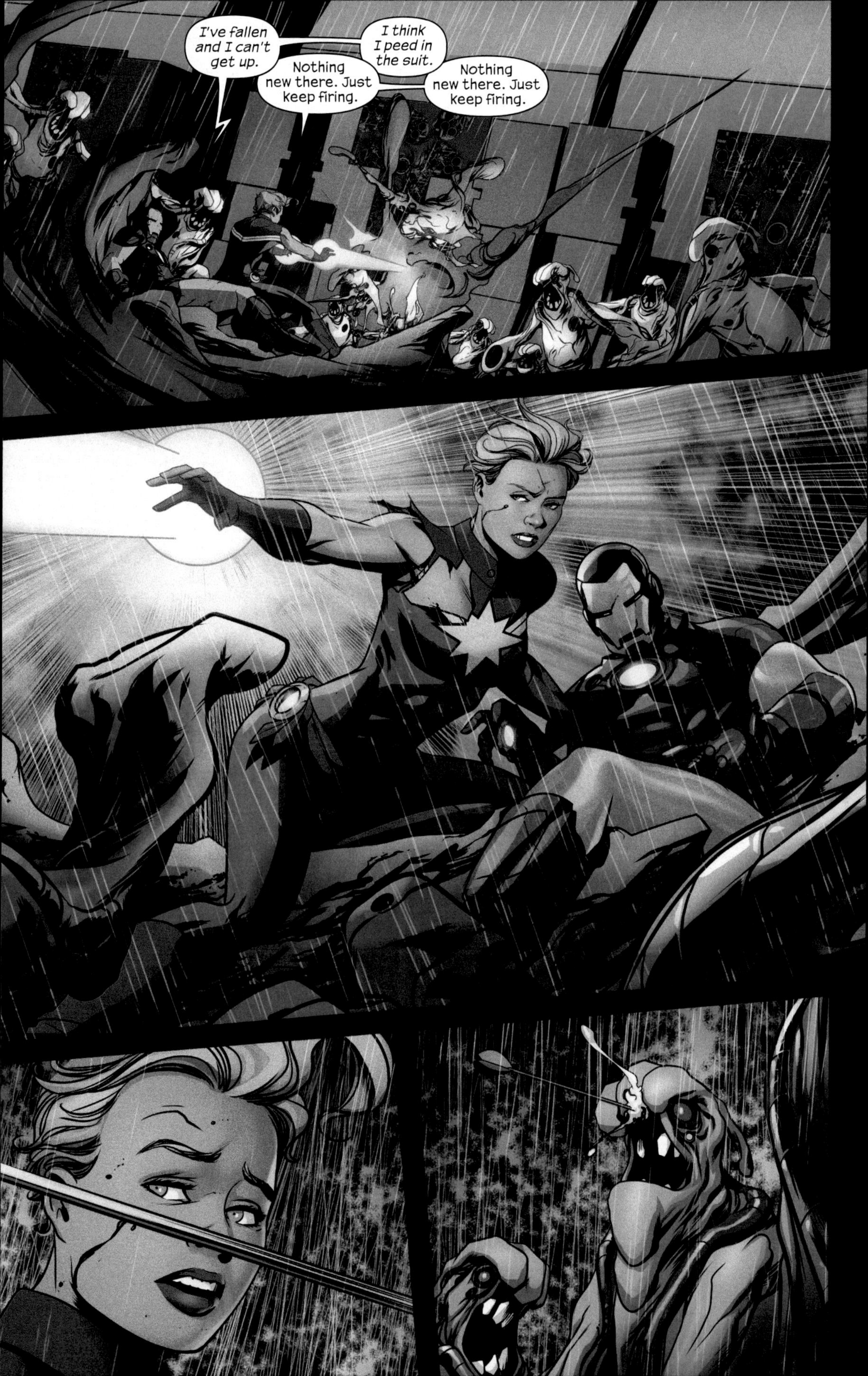
I've fallen and I can't get up.
I think I peed in the suit.
Nothing new there. Just keep firing.
Nothing new there. Just keep firing.

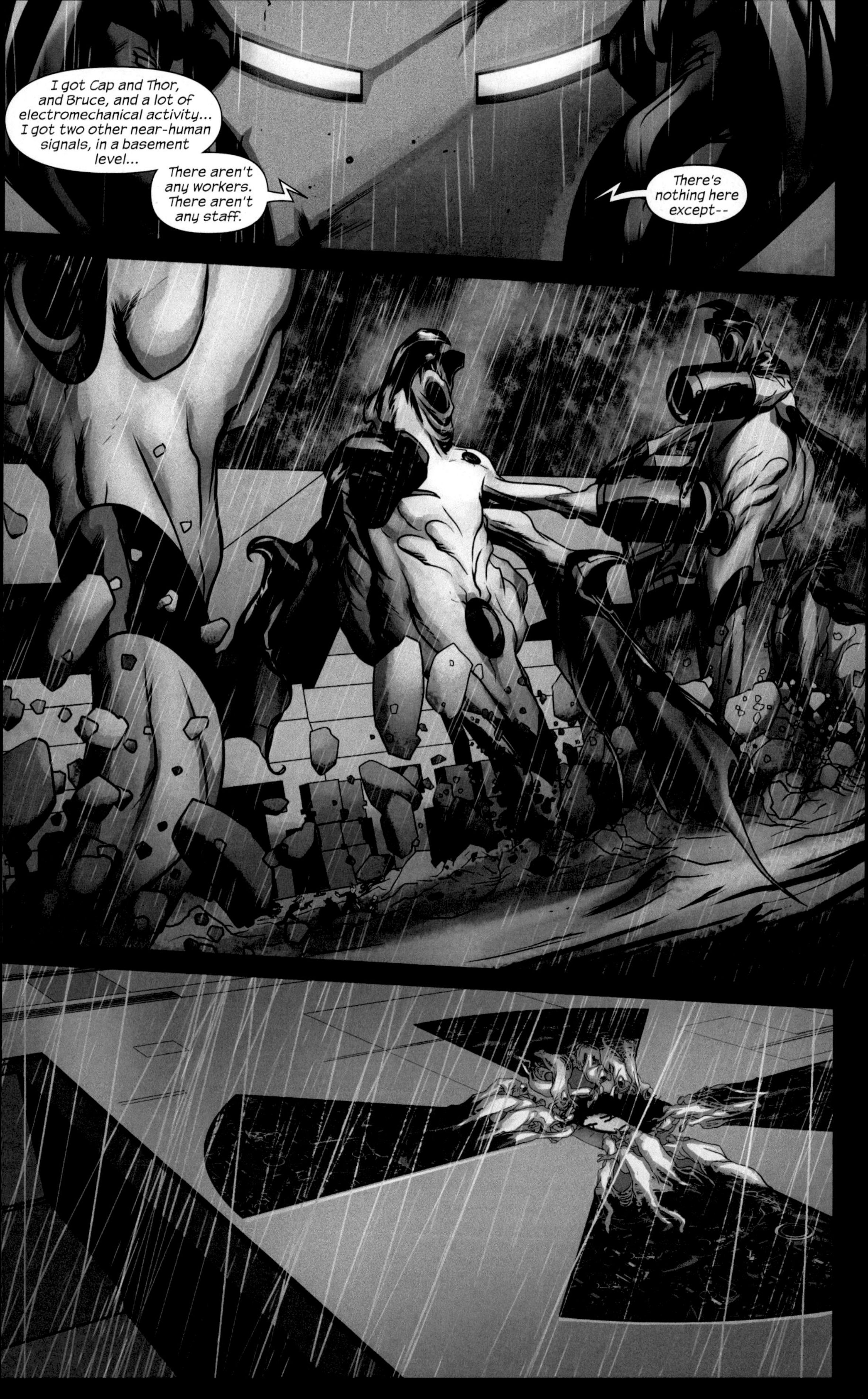
I got Cap and Thor, and Bruce, and a lot of electromechanical activity... I got two other near-human signals, in a basement level...
There aren't any workers. There aren't any staff.
There's nothing here except--

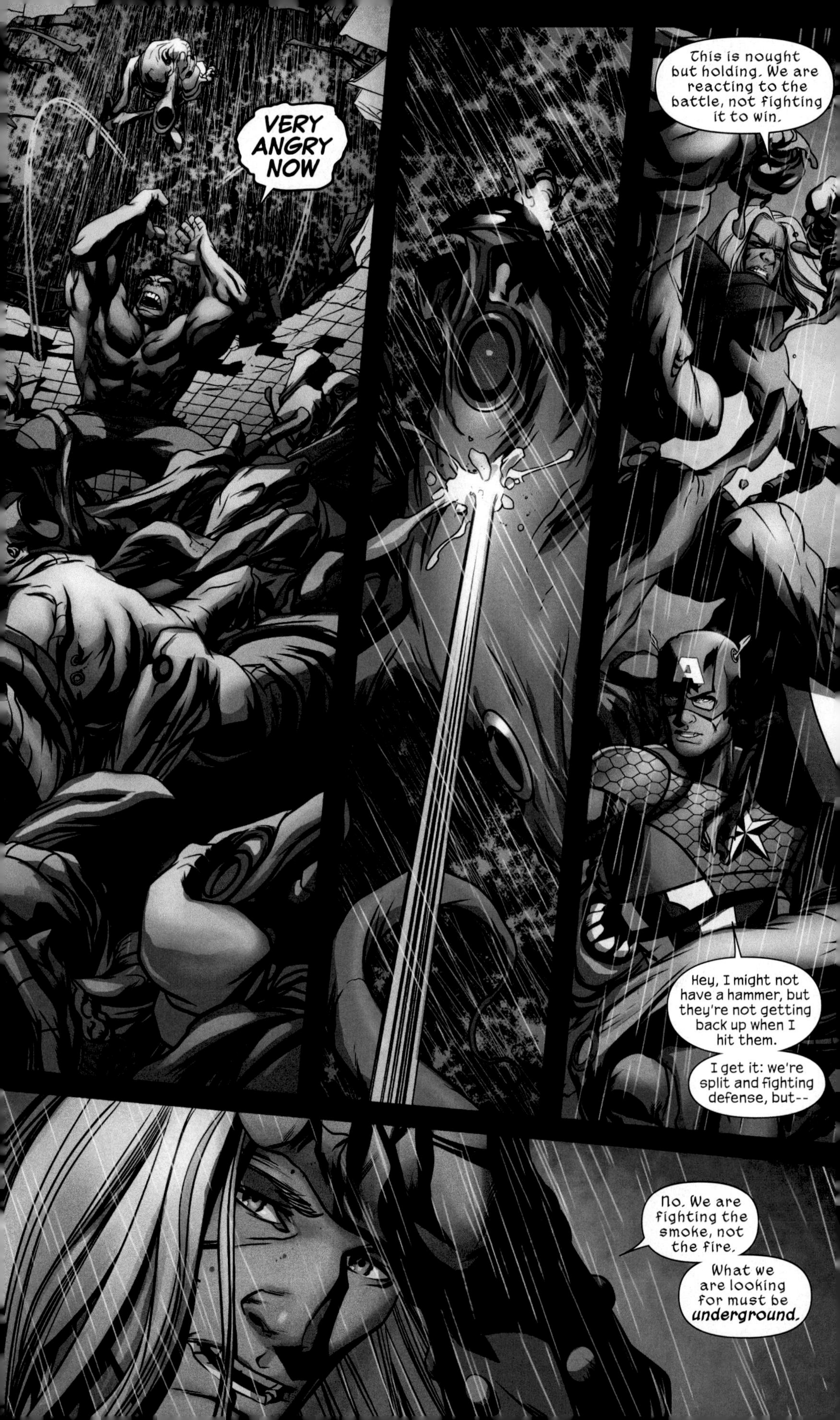

VERY ANGRY NOW
This is nought but holding. We are reacting to the battle, not fighting it to win.
Hey, I might not have a hammer, but they're not getting back up when I hit them.
I get it: we're split and fighting defense, but--
No. We are fighting the smoke, not the fire.
What we are looking for must be *underground.*

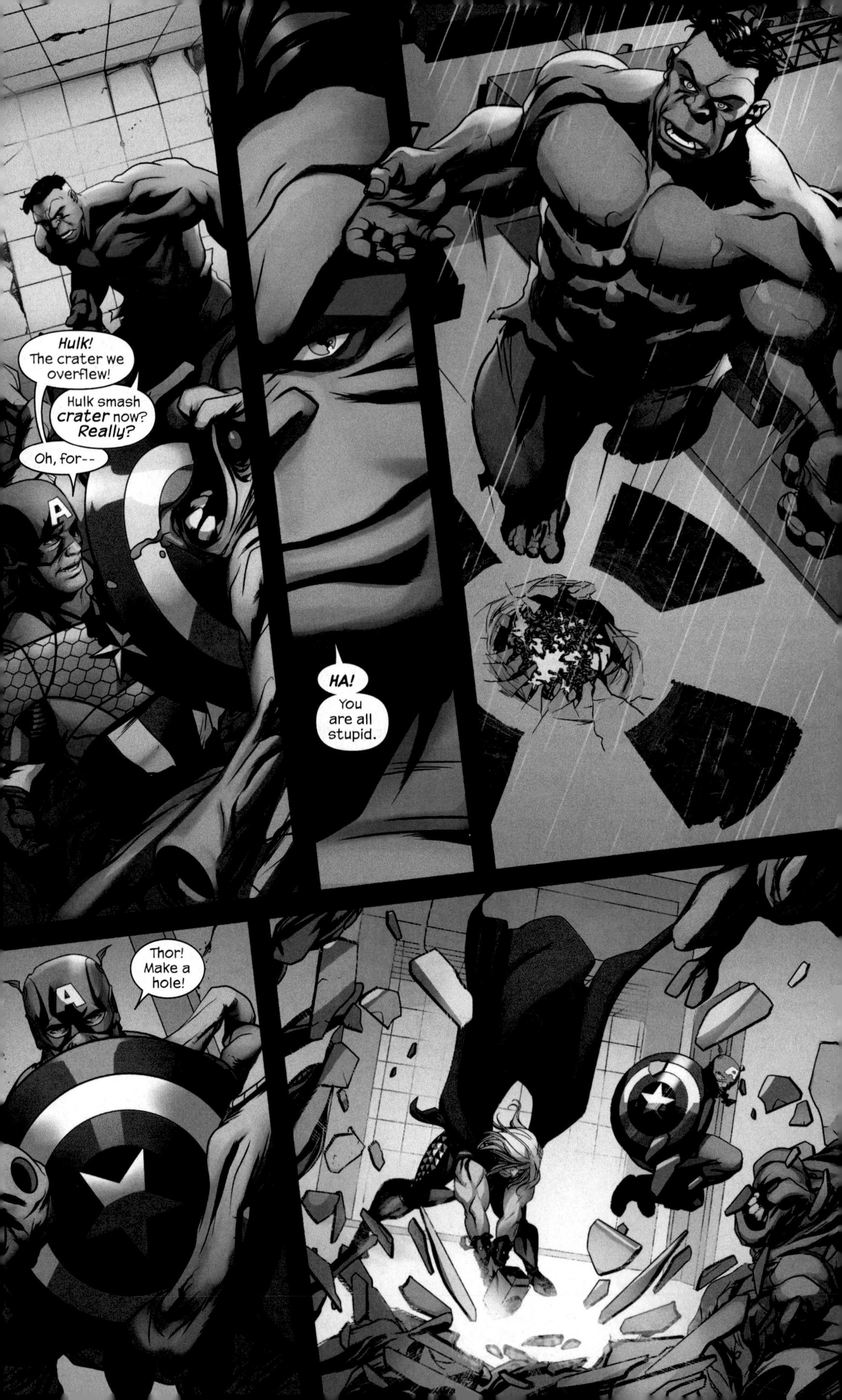

Hulk! The crater we overflew!
Hulk smash crater now? Really?
Oh, for--
HA! You are all stupid.
Thor! Make a hole!

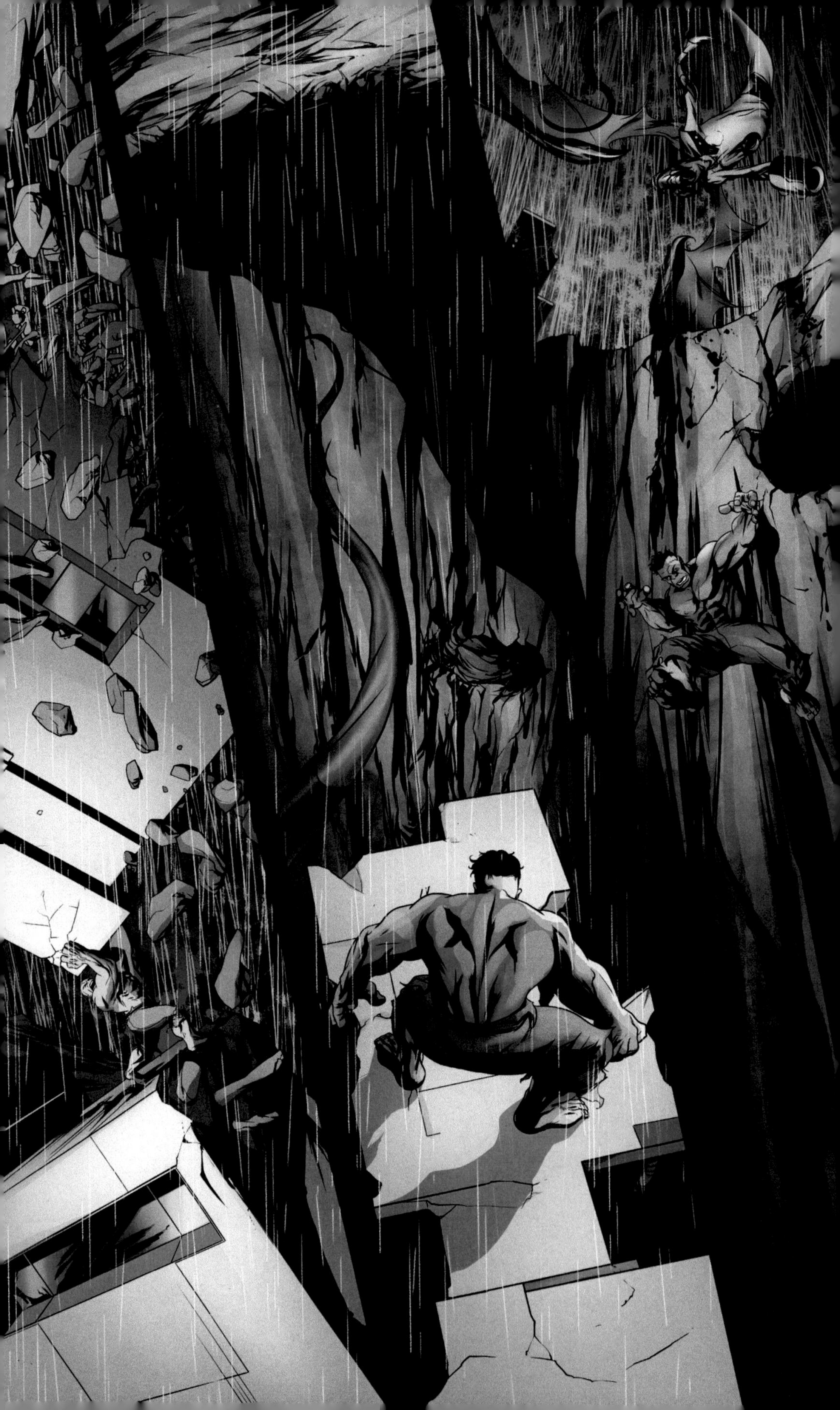

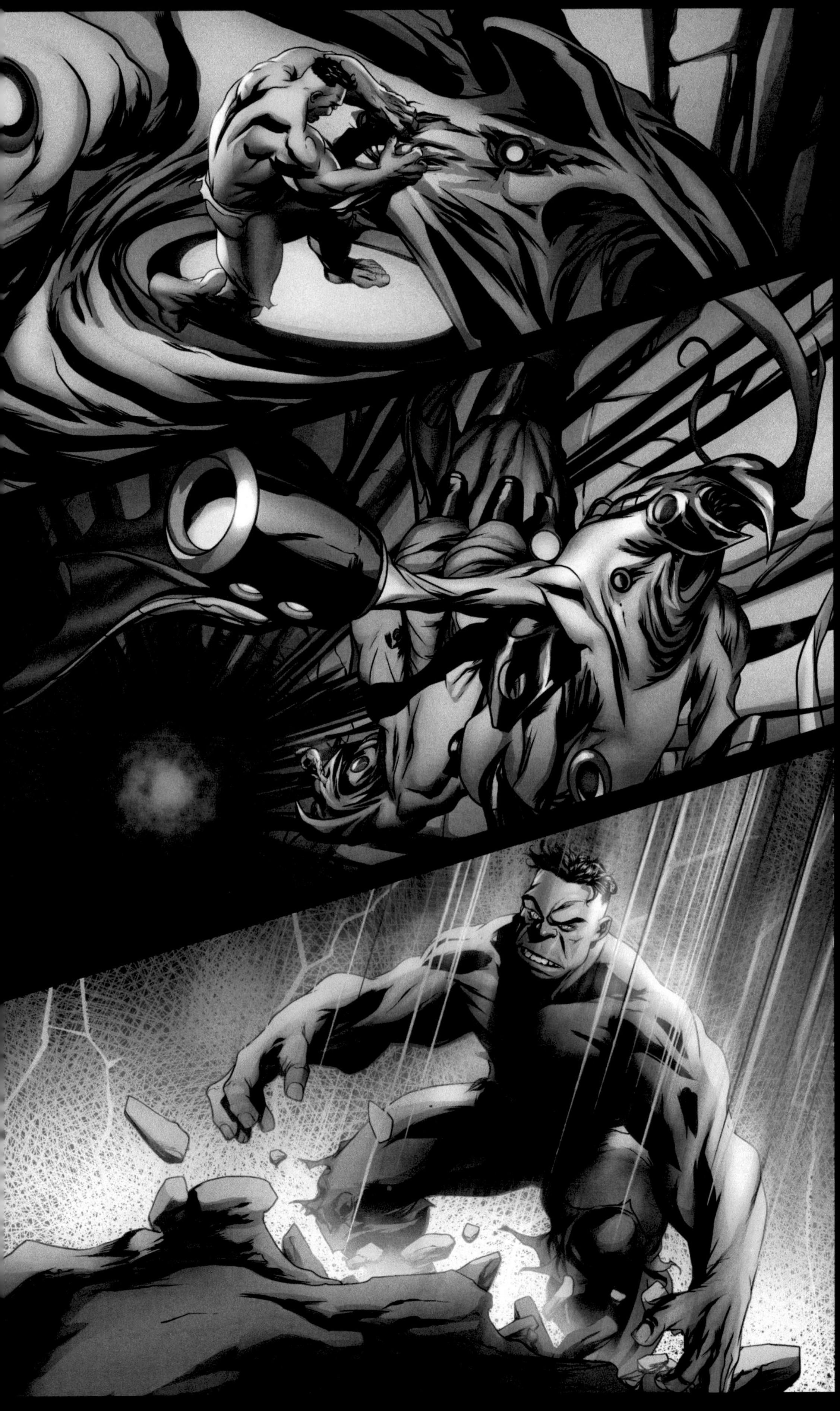

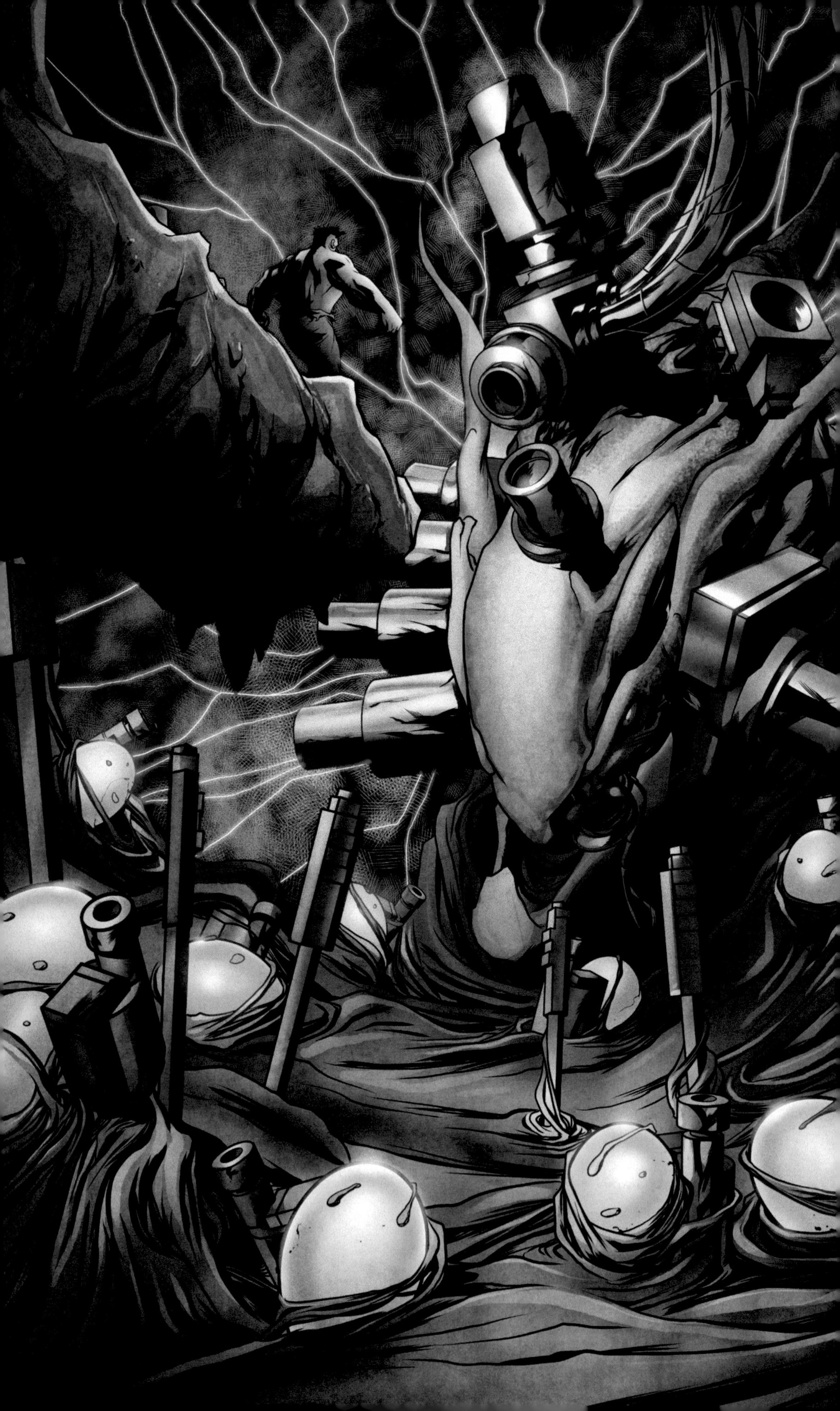

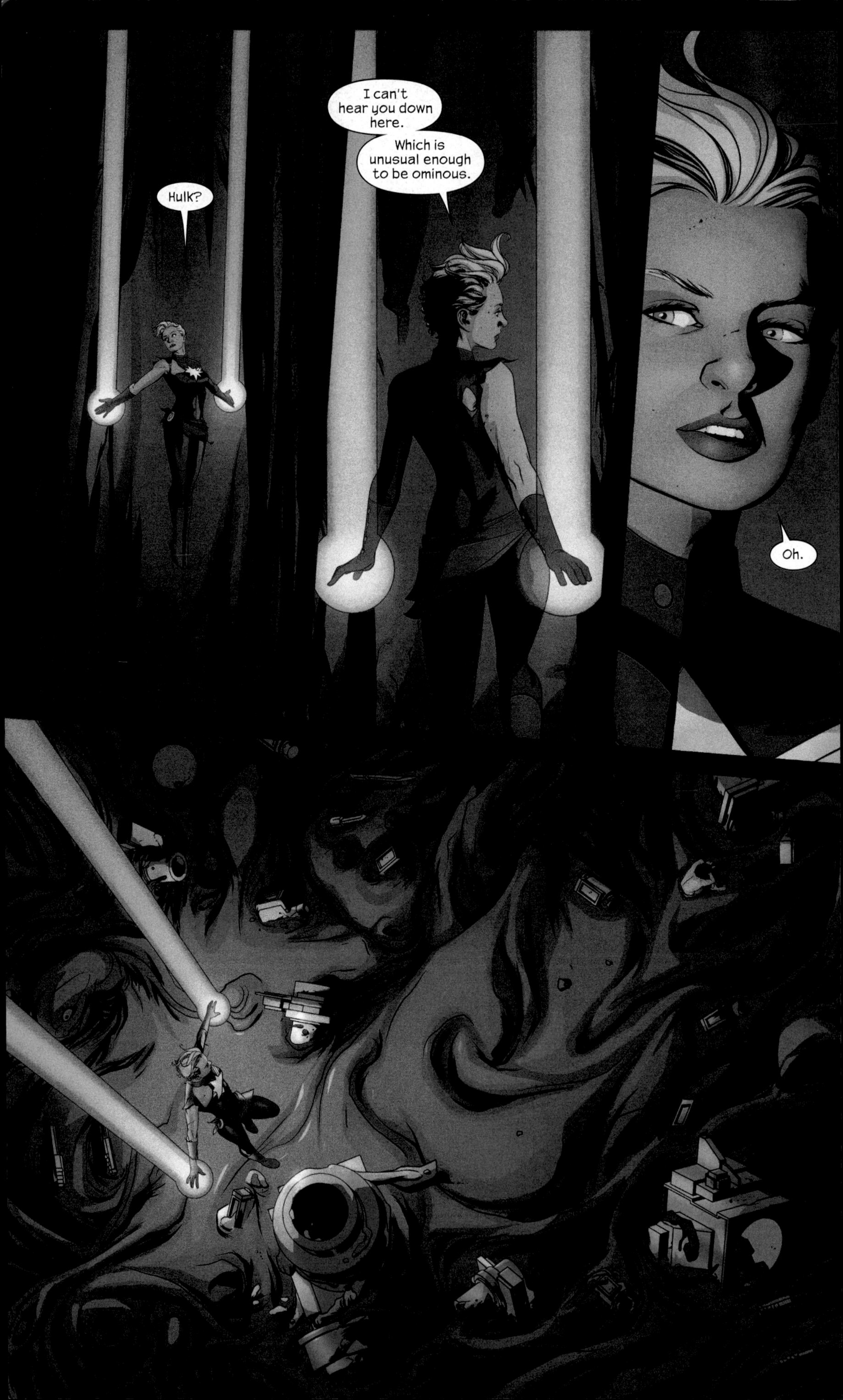
Hulk?
I can't hear you down here.
Which is unusual enough to be ominous.
Oh.

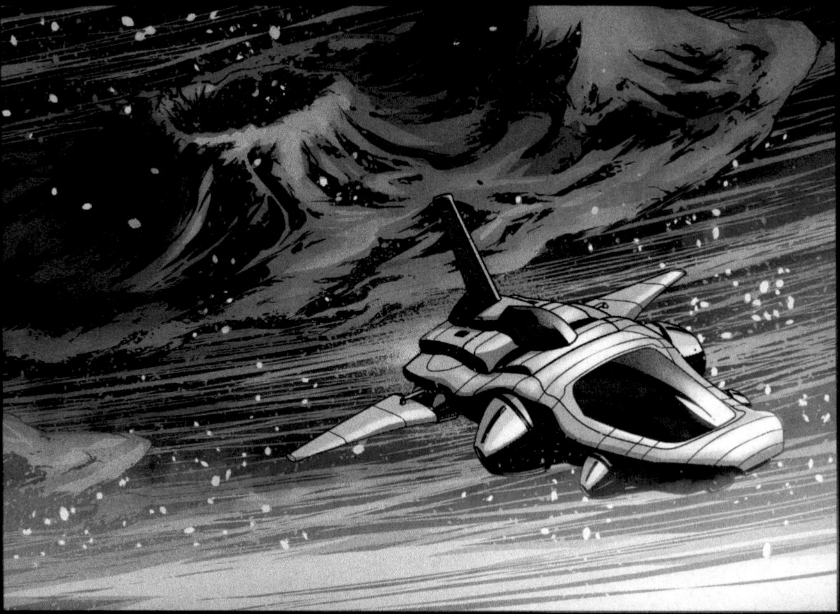

The future is a foreign country. All the things he loved are buried in a century past, and all the things he hated never died. It had occurred to him, more than once, that World War Two was some tarry quicksand that never stopped trying to drag him under the ground where he belonged.

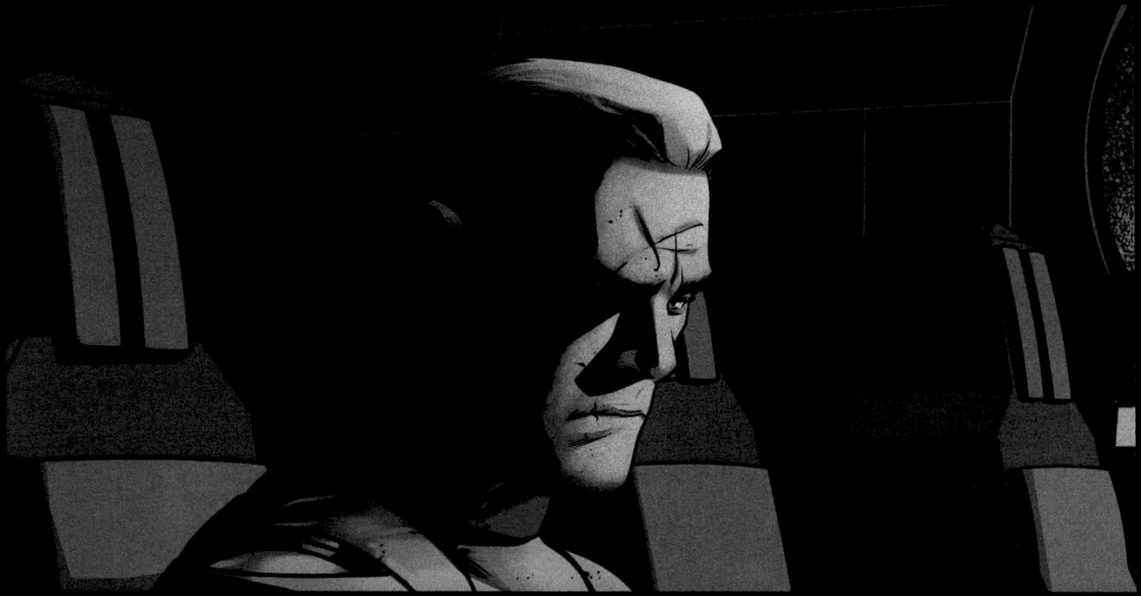

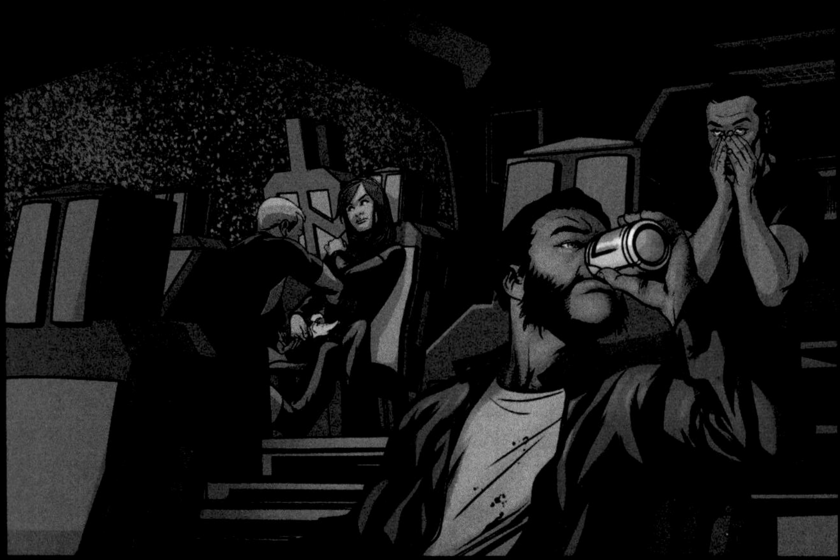

Thor stayed behind. He said he needed to conclude things and make amends. He wore that particular expression that meant, once again, he was returning to that far mythic home of his, and, once again, not as the conquering hero of his dreams.

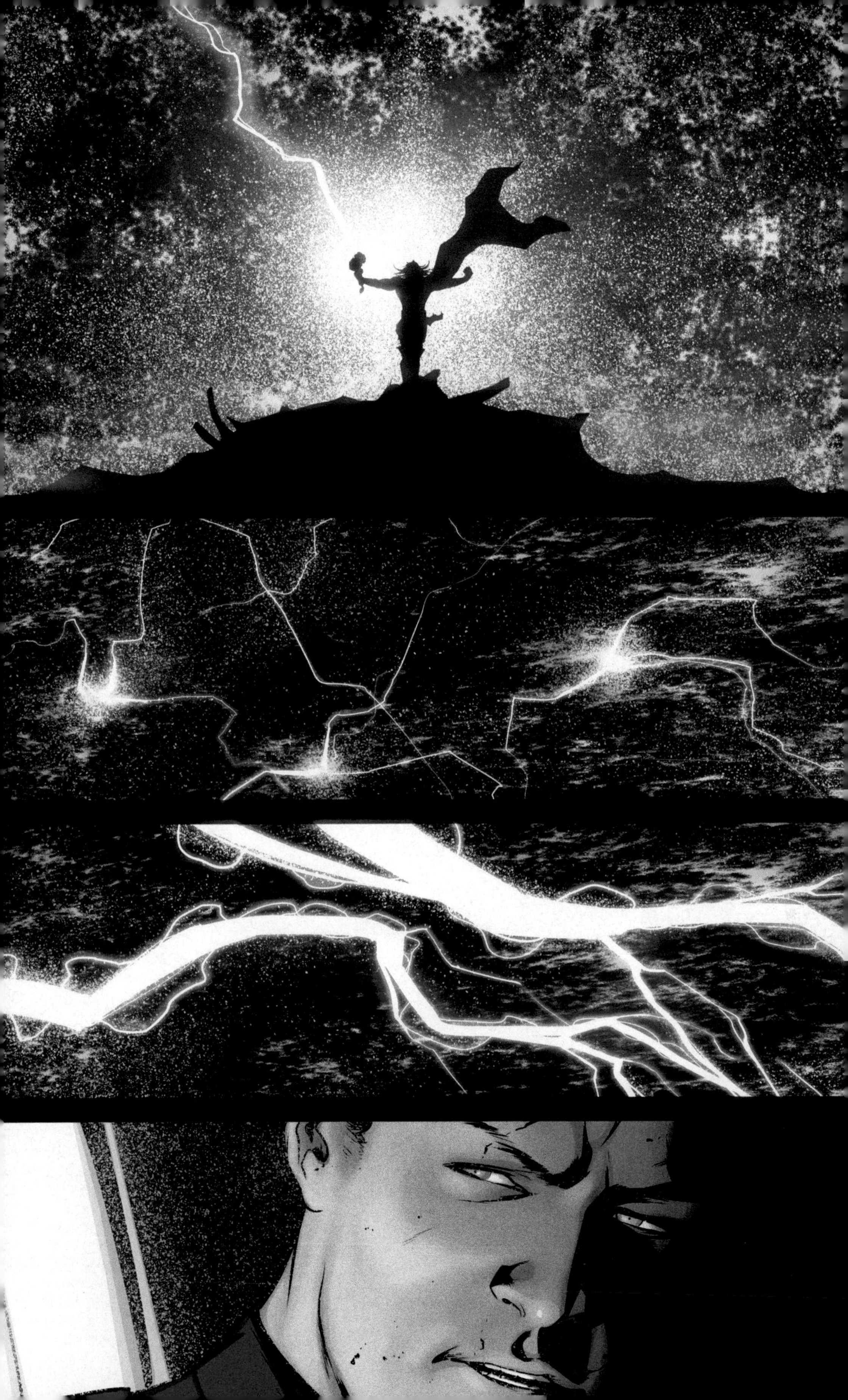

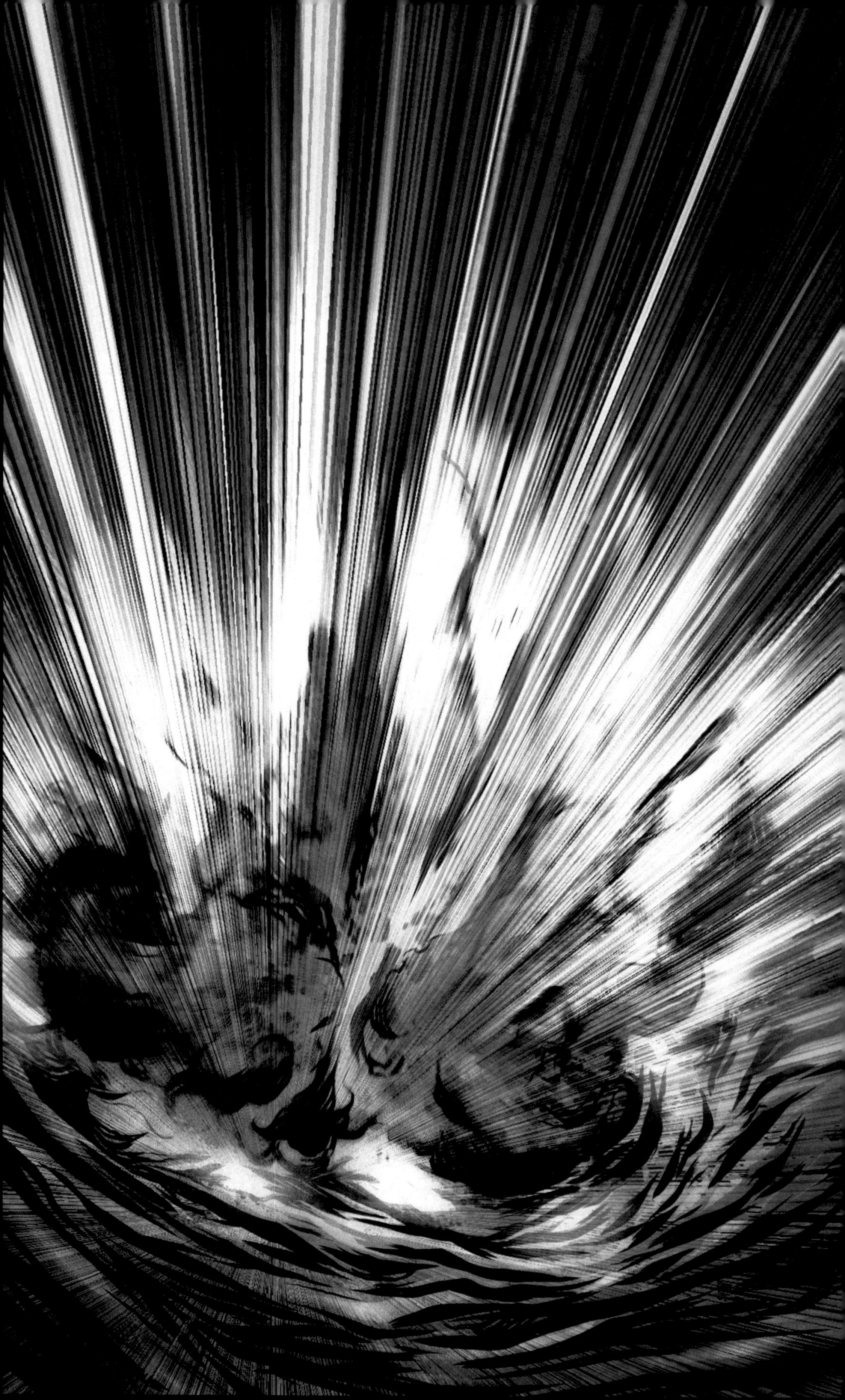

Warren Ellis

Springing from the fertile ground of the U.K. comics scene, Warren Ellis came to Marvel during the early '90s and proved his iconoclastic mettle in the ultra-edgy series *Hellstorm* and the miniseries *Druid* — followed by fondly remembered, extended runs on *Excalibur* and *Doom 2099*. After making a name for himself as a premier talent with Wildstorm's *Stormwatch*, *Transmetropolitan*, *The Authority* and *Planetary*, Ellis returned to Marvel to pen such titles as *Ultimate Fantastic Four*, the *Ultimate Galactus Trilogy* and *Iron Man*. His *Nextwave: Agents of H.A.T.E.* was both a critical smash and cult favorite. In addition to reviving the 1980s *New Universe* in *newuniversal* and writing *Thunderbolts*, Ellis took over *Astonishing X-Men* following Joss Whedon and John Cassaday's departure, and penned perhaps the definitive story of the Armored Avenger in *Iron Man's* "Extremis." His Wildstorm miniseries *Red* was adapted into a 2010 hit movie. Ellis broke into prose fiction with *Crooked Little Vein* and his New York Times best-selling novel *Gun Machine*.

Mike McKone

Artist Mike McKone was pegged as a future industry superstar when his first work was published in DC's *JLA* and *Legion*. In 2001, McKone collaborated with writer Judd Winick to launch Marvel's *Exiles*, a surprise hit among X-fans. Two years later, he teamed with writer Geoff Johns to revamp *Teen Titans* for DC. Since signing an exclusive contract with Marvel, McKone's credits include *Fantastic Four*, *Amazing Spider-Man* and *Avengers Academy*.

Jason Keith

An Eisner Award nominee, Jason Keith has been a colorist in the industry for more than a decade. He got his start at CrossGen coloring *Scion* and *Sojourn;* among his first work at Marvel was writer/artist Frank Cho's *Shanna, the She-Devil.* Since then, he has colored *X-Men, New Avengers, newuniversal, Savage Wolverine* and more.

Chris Eliopoulos

Eagle, Harvey and Wizard Fan Award winner for his lettering, Chris Eliopoulos' prolific career in comics has been anything but the norm. He's worked on dozens of books during the fifteen years he's been in the industry — including Erik Larsen's *Savage Dragon,* for which he hand-lettered the first 100 issues. He's also published his own strips, *Desperate Times* and *Misery Loves Sherman;* been a contributing artist to the *Idiot's Guide To...* series of books; wrote and illustrated Marvel's popular *Franklin Richards: Son of a Genius* one-shots; and penned miniseries featuring *Lockjaw* and the *Pet Avengers.*

Rian Hughes

Designer and illustrator Rian Hughes began his career in the British music, advertising and fashion industries. His strips for *2000AD* and the short-lived *Revolver* with Grant Morrison and Mark Millar are collected in *Yesterday's Tomorrows* and *Tales from Beyond Science*. Designs for Titan Books' *Batman* and *Love and Rockets* volumes brought him to the attention of DC Comics, for whom he has designed numerous logos, including *Batman and Robin*, *Batgirl* and *The Invisibles*. For Marvel he has designed logos and covers for *Iron Man, X-Men* and *Wolverine* among many others. He both wrote and designed the critically acclaimed *Cult-ure: Ideas Can Be Dangerous.*

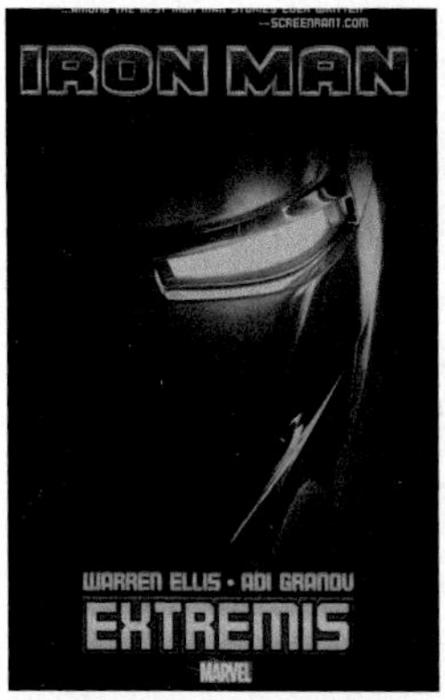

IRON MAN
WARREN ELLIS • ADI GRANOV
EXTREMIS
MARVEL

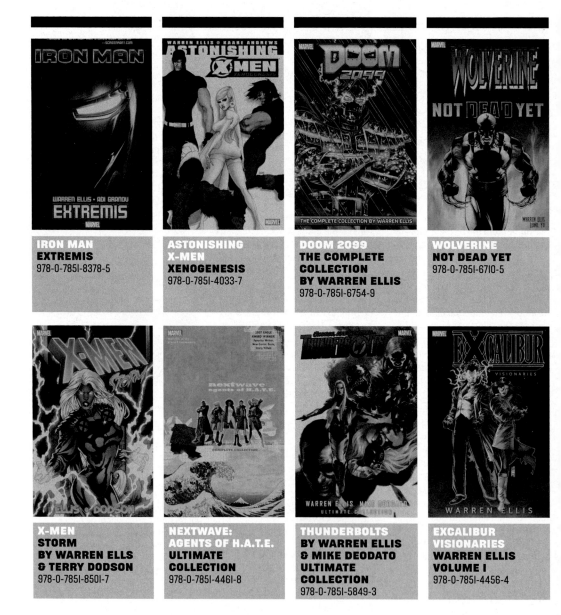

IRON MAN
EXTREMIS
978-0-7851-8378-5

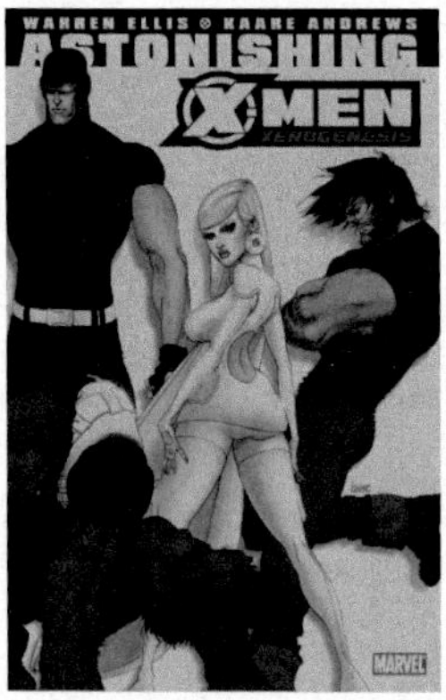

WARREN ELLIS & KAARE ANDREWS
ASTONISHING
X-MEN
XENOGENESIS
MARVEL

ASTONISHING
X-MEN
XENOGENESIS
978-0-7851-4033-7

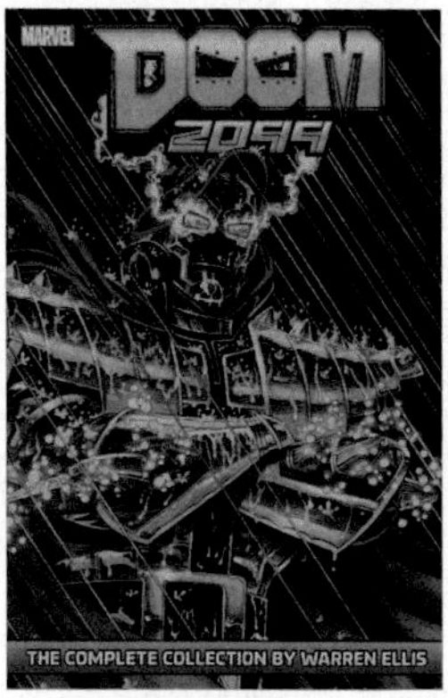

MARVEL
DOOM
2099
THE COMPLETE COLLECTION BY WARREN ELLIS

DOOM 2099
THE COMPLETE
COLLECTION
BY WARREN ELLIS
978-0-7851-6754-9

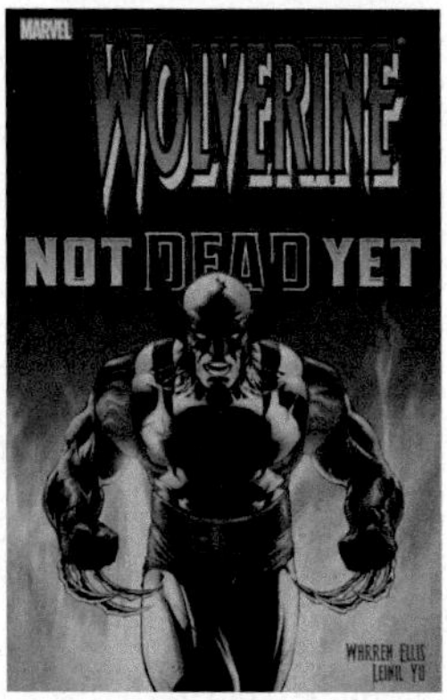

MARVEL
WOLVERINE
NOT DEAD YET
WARREN ELLIS
LEINIL YU

WOLVERINE
NOT DEAD YET
978-0-7851-6710-5

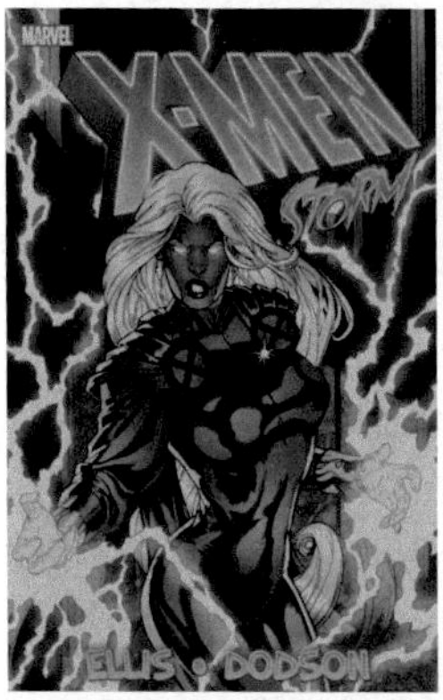

MARVEL
X-MEN
STORM
ELLIS DODSON

X-MEN
STORM
BY WARREN ELLS
& TERRY DODSON
978-0-7851-8501-7

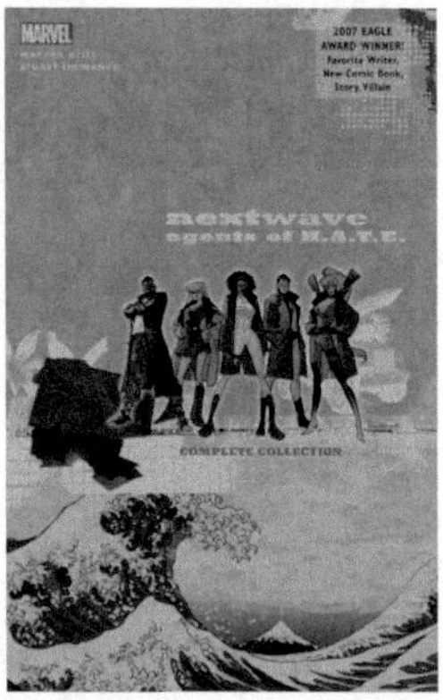

MARVEL
nextwave
agents of H.A.T.E.
COMPLETE COLLECTION

NEXTWAVE:
AGENTS OF H.A.T.E.
ULTIMATE
COLLECTION
978-0-7851-4461-8

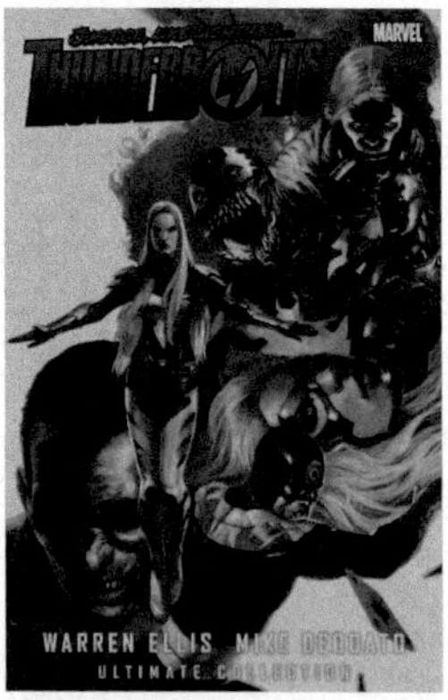

MARVEL
THUNDERBOLTS
WARREN ELLIS MIKE DEODATO
ULTIMATE COLLECTION

THUNDERBOLTS
BY WARREN ELLIS
& MIKE DEODATO
ULTIMATE
COLLECTION
978-0-7851-5849-3

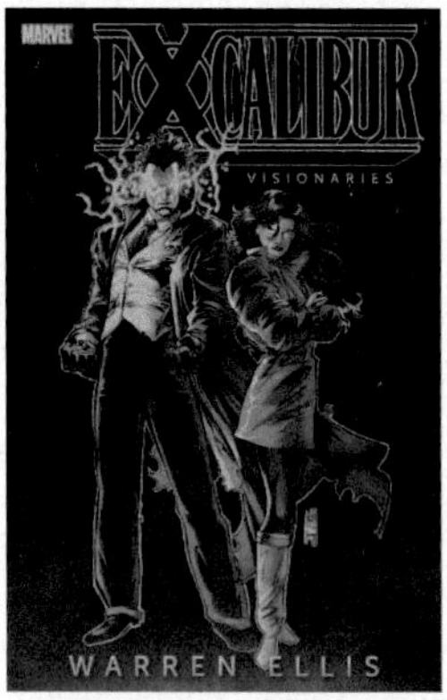

MARVEL
EXCALIBUR
VISIONARIES
WARREN ELLIS

EXCALIBUR
VISIONARIES
WARREN ELLIS
VOLUME 1
978-0-7851-4456-4

He is Karnak of the Inhumans, and he has the fate of humanity in his lethal hands. Will he save it, or end it?

KARNAK VOL. 1: THE FLAW IN ALL THINGS

Collecting *Karnak #1-6*
By Warren Ellis,
Gerardo Zaffino,
Antonio Fuso,
Roland Boschi
and Dan Brown

Coming soon

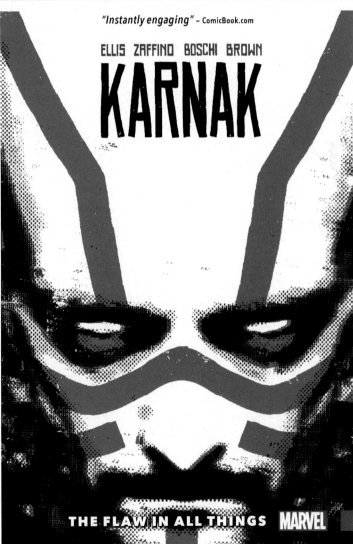

"Instantly engaging" - ComicBook.com
ELLIS ZAFFINO BOSCHI BROWN
KARNAK
THE FLAW IN ALL THINGS
MARVEL